I0454710

U.S. POLICY TOWARD PUTIN'S RUSSIA

HEARING

BEFORE THE

COMMITTEE ON FOREIGN AFFAIRS
HOUSE OF REPRESENTATIVES

ONE HUNDRED FOURTEENTH CONGRESS

SECOND SESSION

JUNE 14, 2016

Serial No. 114–191

Printed for the use of the Committee on Foreign Affairs

Available via the World Wide Web: http://www.foreignaffairs.house.gov/ or
http://www.gpo.gov/fdsys/

U.S. GOVERNMENT PUBLISHING OFFICE

20–454PDF   WASHINGTON : 2016

For sale by the Superintendent of Documents, U.S. Government Publishing Office
Internet: bookstore.gpo.gov   Phone: toll free (866) 512–1800; DC area (202) 512–1800
Fax: (202) 512–2104   Mail: Stop IDCC, Washington, DC 20402–0001

COMMITTEE ON FOREIGN AFFAIRS

EDWARD R. ROYCE, California, *Chairman*

CHRISTOPHER H. SMITH, New Jersey
ILEANA ROS-LEHTINEN, Florida
DANA ROHRABACHER, California
STEVE CHABOT, Ohio
JOE WILSON, South Carolina
MICHAEL T. McCAUL, Texas
TED POE, Texas
MATT SALMON, Arizona
DARRELL E. ISSA, California
TOM MARINO, Pennsylvania
JEFF DUNCAN, South Carolina
MO BROOKS, Alabama
PAUL COOK, California
RANDY K. WEBER SR., Texas
SCOTT PERRY, Pennsylvania
RON DeSANTIS, Florida
MARK MEADOWS, North Carolina
TED S. YOHO, Florida
CURT CLAWSON, Florida
SCOTT DesJARLAIS, Tennessee
REID J. RIBBLE, Wisconsin
DAVID A. TROTT, Michigan
LEE M. ZELDIN, New York
DANIEL DONOVAN, New York

ELIOT L. ENGEL, New York
BRAD SHERMAN, California
GREGORY W. MEEKS, New York
ALBIO SIRES, New Jersey
GERALD E. CONNOLLY, Virginia
THEODORE E. DEUTCH, Florida
BRIAN HIGGINS, New York
KAREN BASS, California
WILLIAM KEATING, Massachusetts
DAVID CICILLINE, Rhode Island
ALAN GRAYSON, Florida
AMI BERA, California
ALAN S. LOWENTHAL, California
GRACE MENG, New York
LOIS FRANKEL, Florida
TULSI GABBARD, Hawaii
JOAQUIN CASTRO, Texas
ROBIN L. KELLY, Illinois
BRENDAN F. BOYLE, Pennsylvania

AMY PORTER, *Chief of Staff*   THOMAS SHEEHY, *Staff Director*
JASON STEINBAUM, *Democratic Staff Director*

CONTENTS

U.S. POLICY TOWARD PUTIN'S RUSSIA

TUESDAY, JUNE 14, 2016

HOUSE OF REPRESENTATIVES,
COMMITTEE ON FOREIGN AFFAIRS,
Washington, DC.

The committee met, pursuant to notice, at 10:11 a.m., in room 2172, Rayburn House Office Building, Hon. Edward Royce (chairman of the committee) presiding.

Chairman ROYCE. The committee will come to order. I will ask all our members to take their seats.

Winston Churchill famously described Russia as "a riddle wrapped in a mystery inside an enigma," but I think for many of us, less well-known is what he said next, because he commented about unlocking that riddle. He said, "But perhaps there is a key. And that key is Russian national interest."

The problem is that we are not dealing with the interests of the Russian people. We could be if we were broadcasting into Russia the way we did during the Reagan administration when we had that message about political pluralism and tolerance and that message of educating people effectively on what was going on inside Russia and around the world. But we don't.

Instead, we are dealing with the interests of Vladimir Putin, because he is in a position there where he is calling the shots. And he has not demonstrated much interest in cooperating with the United States. In fact, many of his policies are directly undermining America—from selling advanced weapons to Iran to destabilizing our allies by sending waves of Syrian refugees, over several million now, across their borders. And for the first time since the end of the Cold War, we have seen a situation where we have been forced to increase our military presence in Europe to make clear our readiness to defend NATO.

Yet, in this environment, Putin continues to escalate. That is why we have this hearing today on our U.S. policy toward Putin's Russia. Over the past year, he has repeatedly sent Russian warplanes to buzz U.S. ships and planes in international waters. These are reckless acts, these are provocative acts, and a miscalculation could easily result in direct confrontation.

As this committee has examined, Russia's propaganda machine—and for any of you who have watched RT television, you can see how it has a constant stream of disinformation that it puts out about the United States, about the U.K., about what actually happens in the world. But that machinery, under Putin, is in overdrive. It is undermining governments, including NATO allies. And, meanwhile, back in Russia, independent media and dissidents are forcefully sidelined. And for the media, when I say "forcibly," I mean imprisoned or sometimes shot.

A big part of the problem is that the administration has repeatedly rushed to try to cooperate with Russia, beginning with a string of one-sided concessions in the New START arms-control agreement. I would just point out, when we pulled out the interceptor system in Poland and in the Czech Republic, I think that was a blunder. We were quick to join diplomatic efforts in Syria, even as the opposition forces we support have come under repeated Russian aerial attack. And this has convinced the Russians that, once again, the administration will concede a great deal for very little in return for the concession.

That does not mean that we should rule out cooperation with Russia. We should cooperate with Russia. But cooperation means benefits for both sides. A tougher and more consistent approach on our part might convince Putin that cooperation is more advantageous than the reflexive confrontation that he often resorts to.

We have clearly demonstrated that we are open to cooperation. It is Putin who is not. And if he continues playing a zero-sum game and regards the U.S. as an enemy to achieving his ends, then the possibility of compromise is zero under that circumstance. Much of his behavior to date fits that description, most glaringly seen by his invasion of Ukraine and what happened in Georgia.

Unfortunately, Putin has repeatedly calculated—rightfully so—that the administration's response to his aggression will be lackluster. The U.S., in cooperation with the EU and others, has imposed sanctions, which have resulted in significant pressure on the Russian economy, but the administration has refused to provide Ukraine, for example, with the anti-tank weaponry needed to stop Russian tanks, which can only be interpreted in Moscow as weakness.

The tragedy is that there are many problems where both countries could benefit from cooperation. One of the most obvious is combating Islamist terrorism. One witness today has intensely studied its rapid spread in Russia and in Central Asia, which, together, provide the largest number of recruits for ISIS outside of the Arab countries.

Putin says he is genuinely concerned about the rising threat. In fact, that was his stated goal in intervening in Syria. But, as we know, his real agenda was to save the Assad regime, which has meant targeting the opposition forces that are supported by the U.S. far more than any targeting of ISIS forces.

It is clear that U.S. strategies to deal with Russia have failed. If we want to accomplish a different result, we must negotiate from a position of strength. Only then will cooperation be possible with a man who has demonstrated that the hope of cooperation cannot survive the cold calculation of his narrow interests.

And one way to address this, to get back to a theme that I have pushed for a number of years here with my colleague Eliot Engel, is the legislation that Eliot and I have advanced to try to get back to a program, as we once had with Radio Free Europe, which we should be doing with social media, with television. We should be broadcasting into Russia, telling Russians what is actually going on in their society, explaining to Russians what is happening around the world, explaining the issue of tolerance, of political pluralism, of these perceptions that the rest of the world have, and the truth.

If Putin is going to continue to put out disinformation and misinformation and lie about the West, at the very least we could be telling the truth about what is happening inside Russia to Russians so that the people have a better understanding of this situation.

I now turn to Ranking Member Eliot Engel of New York for any comments he may have.

Mr. ENGEL. Thank you very much, Mr. Chairman. And let me say I agree with the statement you just made. Thank you for calling this hearing. You and I have long shared deep concerns about Russia's aggression under Vladimir Putin, and I am grateful that you have focused the committee's attention on this challenge.

To all of our witnesses, welcome to the Foreign Affairs Committee. We are grateful for your expertise and insight.

Ambassador McFaul, let me say how particularly impressed I was with your service as our top diplomat in Moscow. I know you were the target of all sorts of absurd accusations and harassment by Putin's allies, and I know that you were never afraid to push back against misinformation and stand your ground. And you are exactly the kind of diplomat we need to meet 21st-century challenges, so thank you for your service.

And the other witnesses, thank you, as well, for your service.

I have come to view Putin's Russia as a unique challenge on the global stage. When we face crises around the world, we often ask ourselves, ''What could we have done differently?'' or, ''What are the opportunities to defuse the situation?'' But, with Putin, there may not be answers to those questions because he is playing by his own set of rules.

Putin has ignored Russian law, cracking down on the human rights of Russia's people and literally robbing future generations of their prosperity. He has destroyed Russia's standing in the world, walking away from the country's international obligations and shoring up the brutal Assad regime in Syria. And he has threatened the norms that have largely kept the peace in Europe since World War II, trampling on the sovereignty of Russia's neighbors, testing the resolve of NATO, and working to undermine Western unity.

I want to be careful not to conflate Putin and his corrupt leadership with the Russian people. Russia is a great nation, but Putin is not Russia. He is an unapologetic, authoritarian kleptocrat, a grave threat to his own people and to stability and security across Europe and beyond.

So how do we craft a policy to deal with such an unpredictable and irresponsible leader? For now, the best approach seems to be one of geographical containment. We cannot fix what is ailing Russian society, but we can try to keep it within Russia's recognized borders.

This may be a great test for NATO's role in the 21st century. NATO, of course, has no ambition to chip away at Russia's territory, but I am confident that the alliance will keep its Article 5 promise. Putin uses lies and confusion to cast doubt on NATO's ability, so I am glad that NATO is ramping up its presence in Eastern Europe, sending a clear signal that the alliance will not back down in the face of Putin's aggression.

I believe and I have said for a long time that I think NATO is being tested. And if we fail the test, I think it the end of the alliance. We cannot fail the test.

Aside from that, sanctions have given us mixed results. As violence in eastern Ukraine escalates again, it is clear that sanctions haven't done enough to thwart Putin's ambitions. But sanctions are better than nothing, and, in the long term, I believe we have weakened Putin's ability to project a destabilizing force beyond Russia's borders.

But we know Putin isn't going anywhere, so we are left to ask, what else should we be doing?

I recently introduced legislation that, in my view, would take us in the right direction. My bill, the STAND for Ukraine Act, would tighten sanctions on Russia and would reject any form of recognition of Russia's rule over Crimea in the same way we didn't recognize Soviet occupation of the Baltic states during the Cold War. It would also help to drive investment in Ukraine and push back against Russian propaganda and disinformation.

There are other issues I hope we can touch on today, as well: How do we help the Russian people hear a different point of view? And the chairman spoke about that in his opening statement. After all, Putin's apparent approval ratings have a lot to do with the fact that there is simply no alternative. How do we seize on the common ground we share with the citizens of Russia? Even if the United States isn't popular in Russia, we know that the country's citizens are disgusted by corruption at every level of government.

And let me close by saying we are not focusing on Russia today because we want to pick a fight, breathe new life into old animosities, or drag the country down. A failed Russia would spread damaging ripple effects around the world. Rather, we hold out hope for the people of Russia. We want to see them realize their democratic aspirations. We want to see their country become a stable and prosperous European power and partner on the world stage. Putin has strangled democracy in Russia. We had such high hopes.

But I look forward to hearing our witnesses today and hearing what they have to say, and I thank them again for coming.

And I yield back, Mr. Chairman.

Chairman ROYCE. All right.

This morning, we are pleased to be joined by a distinguished panel.

The Honorable Michael McFaul is a professor at Stanford University. Prior to his position, Ambassador McFaul served 5 years in the Obama administration, first as Special Assistant to the President and Senior Director for Russia and Eurasia at the National Security Council, and then as the U.S. Ambassador to Russia.

Ambassador Jack Matlock is a fellow at Duke University, and, prior to this position, Ambassador Matlock served 35 years in the American Foreign Service. During that time, he has served as the Ambassador to the Soviet Union, Special Assistant to the President for National Security Affairs, and Ambassador to Czechoslovakia from 1981 to 1983.

Dr. Leon Aron is a resident scholar and director of Russian studies at the American Enterprise Institute. He has served on the Broadcasting Board of Governors since 2015. Prior to these positions, he taught at Georgetown University.

Without objection, the witnesses' full prepared statements will be made part of the record, and our members will have 5 calendar days to submit statements and questions and extraneous material for the record.

Ambassador McFaul, please summarize your remarks, if you could. Thank you, Ambassador.

STATEMENT OF THE HONORABLE MICHAEL MCFAUL, SENIOR FELLOW AND DIRECTOR AT THE FREEMAN SPOGLI INSTITUTE FOR INTERNATIONAL STUDIES, STANFORD UNIVERSITY (FORMER AMERICAN AMBASSADOR TO RUSSIA)

Ambassador MCFAUL. Thank you, Mr. Chairman. Thank you——

Chairman ROYCE. Ambassador, let me just interrupt you. If everyone would push that red button.

Ambassador MCFAUL. Push the top button?

Chairman ROYCE. There you go.

Ambassador MCFAUL. All right? There you go.

So I will thank you again, Chairman Royce and Ranking Member Engel and other members of the committee, including several of you that I had the pleasure of hosting in Moscow when I was Ambassador.

It is great to be back with Ambassador Matlock and Leon Aron, people I know well. I guarantee you, if you listen, you are going to learn something from these two gentlemen today.

I have a longer report that I want to put in the record, but I just want to answer two questions today in the limited time I have: Why did we get here, how did we get here, in terms of this confrontation, which I believe is worse than at any time since the Cold War? In fact, I think you have to go deep into the Cold War to see a time that has been so confrontational. And, as the Russians like to say, "Chto delat," what is to be done.

And I want to focus on the diagnostics first, in part because I am an aspiring professor, recovering bureaucrat, and I think it is important to know the "why" question before you do the prescription. So I am going to first focus on that and, in my limited time, then get to prescriptions.

One argument why we are in this mess that we are in today is that Russia, and Putin in particular, is pushing back after decades of American aggression against him. The United States lectured Russia about markets and democracy, we expanded NATO, we bombed Serbia, we invaded Iraq, we supported color revolutions, so the argument goes, and so Putin just had to push back; he was compelled to annex Crimea and intervene in eastern Ukraine. And most certainly that is the main conflict that has sparked the confrontation.

Now, I want to be clear. None of those policies were popular in Moscow during the last three decades, although it should be noted that both President Yeltsin and Putin at one point flirted with the idea of actually joining NATO.

But in between that negative record that I just described and our moment today, there was a period of cooperation. We in the Obama administration called it the ''reset.'' And, during that period, we got a lot of things done that, Mr. Chairman, in my opinion, were in the American national interests. We got the START Treaty done. We got sanctions on Iran. We expanded the northern distribution network to supply our troops in Afghanistan so we had an alternative route instead of Pakistan, which was vital to a military mission we had in 2011 when we killed Osama bin Laden. We got them into the World Trade Organization. We got them to support U.N. Security Council Resolutions 1970 and 1973 on Libya. And we increased trade and investment during that period. By the way, during this period, 60 percent of Americans thought Russia was a friendly or allied country, and vice versa inside Russia.

That was just 4 years ago. That wasn't 40 years ago or before the Bolshevik revolution. So you can't explain the period of cooperation that I just described looking at these previous variables. Something else has to be here.

A second explanation is that Obama was weak and created the permissive conditions for Putin's aggression. Maybe we will have time to talk about that in questions and answers in more detail.

I would just remind you that every time a Russian leader has decided to use force or to suppress democratic movements in Eastern Europe, the United States has not had good options for deterring it. Whether it is in Georgia in 2008 under George W. Bush, the crackdown on Solidarity in 1981 under Ronald Reagan, 1968 in Czechoslovakia, or 1966 in Hungary, we did not have military means for stopping them.

Let me say something really provocative. I believe the Obama administration's response looks more like Ronald Reagan's response to what happened in Poland in 1981 than George Bush's response to what happened in Georgia in 2008. That did get your attention, didn't it? I will bet you we are going to come back with that.

The third explanation, and what I think is the real driving explanation for what is going on, is this is all about domestic politics in Russia and in Ukraine and very little to do with American foreign policy, either strong or weak. Two things are important to this explanation. One, Putin returned. And Putin is not Medvedev. He sees the world in zero-sum terms. He sees the hand of the CIA in fomenting revolutions in the Arab world, in Ukraine, and in Russia. And he sees us fundamentally as an enemy. And, second, there were giant demonstrations against his regime in December 2011 and in the spring of 2012 when I was Ambassador, and he needed a new argument to suppress those people, to say that they were the enemies of the regime. And that is when he rolled out this old playbook from the Soviet era and described us—the United States, the Obama administration, and me personally—as the enemy, those that are fomenting revolution against him.

And, in that context, there is not an easy way to cooperate with him if he sees the world in these zero-sum terms and if he sees an American hand behind these uprisings, be they in Moscow or Kiev.

So, to me, I actually agree with both the previous statements. It is a tragic moment in U.S.-Russian relations; I don't celebrate this at all. But we have to have a patient, comprehensive policy for deterring Russian aggression, working with the government when it is in our national interest, and supporting Russian society.

In my written remarks, I go into detail about a six-point plan. Let me just mention the headlines and then stop. One, most important of all, in my opinion, to deter Putin's aggression, is to help Ukrainian democracy and markets succeed. Nothing else is more important than that objective, and so I look forward to seeing your legislation. I think that is orders of magnitude more important than anything else. Second, strengthening NATO, as has already been noted. I fully concur with that. Third, pushing back on Russian propaganda, not through American propaganda but through facts. I agree with that. Fourth, working with the government in limited ways when we can, when it serves our national interest. And, finally, engaging in supporting the Russian people, because there is no reason to contain both the state and the people. We should continue to engage when the circumstances allow.

Thank you, Mr. Chairman.

[The prepared statement of Ambassador McFaul follows:]

Testimony of Michael McFaul

Director of the Freeman Spogli Institute for International Studies, Stanford University

U.S. House Foreign Affairs Committee Hearing: "U.S. Policy Towards Putin's Russia."
June 14, 2016

Michael McFaul is the Director of the Freeman Spogli Institute for International Studies, Senior Fellow at the Hoover Institution, and Professor of Political Science all at Stanford University. He served five years in the Obama administration, first as Special Assistant to the President and Senior Director for Russia and Eurasia at the National Security Council (2009-2012) and then as the U.S. Ambassador to the Russian Federation (2012-2014). Twitter: @McFaul.

U.S.-Russia relations today are more strained and more confrontational than at any time since the end of the Cold War. In fact, even some periods of the Cold War seemed more cooperative than our current era. For the first time since the end of the World War II, a European country has annexed territory of a neighbor. Emboldened by the relative ease of Crimea's annexation, Vladimir Putin then went a step further and intervened in eastern Ukraine in an attempt to wrestle more territory away from Kiev's control. Inside Russia, Putin has increased his autocratic grip, in part by blaming the United States for "fomenting revolution" against his regime. Once again, like the darkest days of the Cold War, Russian stated-controlled media outlets portray the United States as Russia's number one enemy intent on weakening if not even dismembering Russia. According to the Kremlin's media, we are also responsible for many of the evils in other countries including the tragic civil wars in Syria and Libya and the Nazis who came to power in Kyiv. As someone who lived in the Soviet Union, I find the current level of vitriol against the United States and the West more generally even worse than during the Cold War days.

The Obama administration's response to these Russian actions, in partnership with American allies in Europe, has been qualitatively different than any other period in the post -Cold War era. Dozens of Russian officials and companies are now sanctioned. Even during the most difficult periods of the Cold War, the chief of staff in the Kremlin was not on a sanctions list. In parallel, after decades of focus on other missions, NATO is now retrained again on deterring a threat from Russia. Two years ago, in his address to the United Nations General Assembly, President Obama argued that the three greatest threats to the world were Ebola, ISIS, and Russia.

In parallel to these actions and reactions between our two governments, majorities of Russians and Americans now view each other again as enemies.

What a tragedy. For last three decades, American presidents -- Democrats and Republicans alike -- sought to integrate Russia into the West and in parallel encourage democracy inside Russia. Both of those projects are now over.

How did we get to this point? What must be done now to pursue American national interests in our relations with Russia?

Diagnosis: The Domestic Sources of Russian Foreign Policy

Too often, we in the United States jump to the discussion of "what must be done" before properly diagnosing the problem. In the case of U.S.-Russia relations, we will only develop successful policy prescriptions if we accurately understand the causes of our current conflict with Russia. Getting the diagnosis wrong can lead to bad policy prescriptions.

One popular explanation of our current confrontation in Moscow and in some circles in Europe and the United States is that the United States and our allies in Europe have been pressing on Russia too hard for too many decades and Putin just had to push back. We lectured the Russians about markets and democracy, then expanded NATO, then bombed Serbia, then invaded Iraq, then allegedly supported color revolutions and the Arab Spring, and Putin finally felt compelled to strike back by annexing Crimea and intervening in eastern Ukraine, or so the argument goes. This explanation is wrong.

Although both Presidents Yeltsin and Putin both suggested that Russia should consider joining NATO at one point in their careers, NATO expansion was never popular in Moscow. Nor did most Russian officials support the NATO campaign against Milosevic, the Bush administration's invasion of Iraq, or so-called color revolutions in Serbia, Georgia, and Ukraine. Yet, these older policy differences cannot be cited to explain our current confrontation, because in between them and today, we had an intense and successful period of cooperation with Russia. We in the Obama administration called it the Reset. During the era of the Reset, from 2009-2012, President Obama and Russian President Medvedev worked together on several projects, which improved the security and prosperity of both countries. In this period, our two countries signed and then ratified the New Start Treaty, passed in the spring of 2010 United Nations Security Council Resolution 1929, the most comprehensive set of sanctions against Iran ever, and developed the Northern Distribution Network (NDN)—a mix of air, rail, and truck routes through Russia and other countries in Central Asia and the Caucuses to supply U.S. soldiers in Afghanistan and reduce U.S. military dependency on the southern route through Pakistan. Our two governments also worked together to diffuse tensions in the Caucuses, and manage ethnic strife in Kyrgyzstan after the government there was toppled. In 2011, President Medvedev even agreed to abstain on UN Security Council Resolutions 1970 and 1973, which authorized the use of force against the Libyan regime of Muammar Gaddafi. No Russian leader had ever acquiesced to a UN-approved military intervention into a sovereign country. In this period, our two governments cooperated to increase trade and investment, including working together to help Russia obtain membership in the World Trade Organization (WTO).

During this period, NATO expansion was not a contentious issue in our bilateral relations. On the contrary, when President Medvedev attended the NATO summit in Lisbon in November 2010, he echoed other Western leaders in waxing effusively about NATO–Russia relations. "Incidentally," he said, "even the declaration approved at the end of our talks states that we seek to develop a strategic partnership. This is not a chance choice of words, but signals that we have succeeded in putting the difficult period in our relations behind us now."[i] Behind closed doors, President Medvedev engaged in a serious discussion with his NATO counterparts on missile defense cooperation.

During the heyday of the Reset, roughly 60% of Americans viewed Russia as a friendly country; a similar number of Russians had a positive view of the United States.

All of this cooperation, all of these positive attitudes towards each other's country, occurred after NATO expansion, after the Iraq War, and after the Orange Revolution in Ukraine. These factors, therefore, cannot be cited to explain the current era of confrontation.

A second explanation also places the blame on the United States, but for doing too little, not too much. Putin invaded Ukraine because Obama was weak, so the argument goes. Former House Speaker John Boehner succinctly expressed this kind of analysis when he said on October 27, 2014,

> "When you look at this chaos that's going on, does anybody think that Vladimir Putin would have gone into Crimea had George W. Bush been president of the United States? No! Even Putin is smart enough to know that Bush would have punched him in the nose in about 10 seconds."

In fact, in response to Putin's more belligerent policies, the Obama Administration began to pivot away from cooperation with Russia long before Putin intervened in Ukraine, including most dramatically cancelling a summit planned in Moscow in September 2013. The truth of the matter, however, is that the United States has never had effective policy options to deter Russian aggression in its neighborhood. Putin actually did invade a neighbor, Georgia, during the Bush administration in August 2008, and President Bush did not punch him in the nose or stop that intervention. Nor did President Ronald Reagan prevent the Soviet-inspired crackdown on Solidarity in December 1981. Likewise, President Johnson could not stop Brezhnev from intervening Czechoslovakia in 1968, and President Eisenhower failed to prevent Soviet tanks from rolling into Hungary in 1956. Whether Democrat or Republican, no U.S. president has ever succeeded in deterring Soviet/Russian military intervention in Eastern Europe in those countries not members of NATO.

The driving force of our current clash with Russia is not American policies, but domestic politics in Russia and Ukraine, specifically Putin's response to popular challenges to his authority and the authority of his former ally in Kyiv. These are forces over which the United States had little control.

Relations with Russia began to deteriorate rapidly after Putin's return to the Kremlin in 2012 and his decision to suppress popular opposition to his rule. In December 2011, tens of thousands of Russian protested against a falsified parliamentary election. Not since 1991 -- the year that the Soviet Union collapsed -- had so many Russian mobilized on the streets against the government. Putin's old social contract – economic growth in return for political passivity – was no longer sufficient to appease these middle class protestors. He needed a new argument for legitimacy, so he turned against the United States, labeling us again as Russia's enemy and calling those demonstrating against him American agents. In particular, Putin argued that the United States was seeking to topple his regime. Like the old days, the United States was interfering in Russia's internal affairs, "We know, regrettably, that…some representatives of some foreign states are gathering those to whom they are paying money, so-called grant recipients, carrying out instruction sessions with them and preparing them to do the relevant 'work', in order to influence, ultimately, the election campaign process in our country."[ii] Putin, his aides, and his media outlets accused the leaders of Russian demonstrations of being U.S. agents. While I was ambassador, these same media outlets constantly propagated the idea that President Obama sent me to Moscow to foment a "color revolution" against Putin's regime. President Putin and his government also blamed the United States for fostering instability and regime change in the Arab world.

During this period, U.S. policy towards Russia did not change. Rather, Putin's policy towards the United States changed radically.

Putin also blamed the United States for fostering regime change against his ally, President Yanukovich, in the fall of 2013. Putin always sees the hidden hand of the CIA behind popular protests since, in his view, individuals cannot act on their own. When Yanukovich fled Ukraine in February 2014, after a desperate effort by Western intermediaries to forge a compromise between the Ukrainian government and the protestors, Putin blamed the United States again. To exact revenge against the new government in Kyiv as well as the "double-crossing" West, he first annexed Crimea and then intervened in the Donbas in support of secessionist groups there.

Two years later, Putin intervened in Syria to make sure his ally, Mr. Assad, did not suffer the same fate as Mr. Yanukovich in Ukraine. Putin's intervention in Syria had everything to do with propping up Assad and very little to do with fighting ISIS.

Putin's intervention in Ukraine was initially very popular among Russians. Putin's perceived success among Russians in battling neo-Nazis in Ukraine, the evil

Americans, and the decadent West more generally will make it hard for him to change course. To maintain his argument for legitimacy at home, Putin needs perpetual conflict with external enemies—not full-scale war or a direct clash with the United States or NATO -- but a low-level, yet constant confrontation to support the narrative that Russia is under siege from the West.

Prescription: Stay the Course

If my explanation for our new confrontation with Russia is correct, then certain policy prescriptions should be followed and others avoided.

Above all else, this conflict did not start as a result of a particular U.S. foreign policy action, so seeking to "correct" some U.S. foreign policy will not produce a change in U.S.-Russian relations. For instance, Putin did not intervene in Ukraine to stop NATO expansion, because NATO expansion to Ukraine was not on the agenda in 2014. Likewise, the United States cannot stop promoting regime change in Russia as a way to win favor with Putin, because the Obama administration was never and is not today promoting regime change in Russia. Equally dangerous would be to forget about Putin's actions in Ukraine and pivot to start making deals with the Kremlin, as Mr. Donald Trump, the Republican Party's presumptive nominee for the November 2016 presidential election, has suggested. Such a policy would prove to Putin and his government that they can annex territory, use military force, and the wait patiently until the United States and Europe grows tired of confrontation and seek cooperation again. Suggesting moral equivalency between Russian behavior and American actions abroad is also very damaging to our national interests. For instance, when Donald Trump says, "well, we are doing a lot of killing ourselves …" in response to a question from MSNBC's Joe Scarborough about Putin's policies, he hands the Russian leader a public relations win.

Instead of searching for corrections in our past policies, we need to stay the course with our current polices. The Obama administration, together with our European allies, responded correctly to Putin's belligerent actions in Ukraine. Obama outlined the stakes at play in his speech in Tallinn on September 2, 2014, explaining that Russian intervention in Ukraine "is a brazen assault on the territorial integrity of Ukraine -- a sovereign and independent European nation. It challenges that most basic of principles of our international system -- that borders cannot be redrawn at the barrel of a gun; that nations have the right to determine their own future. It undermines an international order where the rights of peoples and nations are upheld and can't simply be taken away by brute force. This is what's at stake in Ukraine. This is why we stand with the people of Ukraine today."[iii] The West's unified and comprehensive response to Putin's aggression was impressive and effective, but now needs to be maintained and deepened.

Support Ukrainian Reform

Putin is waiting for Ukrainian economic and political reform to fail. Our goal must to do all that we can to help Ukrainian reform succeed. There is no better way to rebuff Putin's belligerent foreign policies and autocratic domestic practices than to consolidate democracy and strengthen market practices in Ukraine.

Under difficult circumstances, the Ukrainian government has achieved success. In close cooperation with the IMF, the Ukrainian government has reduced government expenditures, raised heating tariffs, tightened monetary policy, and eliminated energy dependence on Russia -- all difficult but important reforms for stimulating again economic growth.

Ukrainian military reform and expanded training also continues, supported by American assistance. The $600 million in security assistance that the United States has committed to Ukraine has increased the effectiveness of Ukrainian military forces to deter future Russian offensives. This support must be continued.

Ukraine's new leaders also have proven capable of enacting major institutional reform. For instance, the overhaul of the police patrolling system, aided by support from the State Department's Bureau of International Narcotics and Law Enforcement Affairs (INL), has been remarkably successful. Ukrainian civil society remains robust, and continues to pressure the government to maintain momentum on reform. U.S. support for Ukrainian civil society has been a smart, impactful investment.

At the same time, more needs to be done. Above all else, the influence of Ukrainian big business conglomerates in politics needs to be reduced. The new government has to make more credible commitments to fighting corruption. U.S. policy should assist them in making these commitments, through aid conditionality, technical assistance, and political support.

The United States and our European allies also should be doing more to reach out, nurture, and support directly the people in the Donbas, including the 1-1.5 million of them currently displaced in other parts of Ukraine. They need short-term humanitarian assistance, as well as long-term support—education, housing, and retraining—to rebuild their futures.

Strengthen NATO

The probability of a Russian attack of a NATO ally is low. Putin does not have a master plan to recreate the Soviet Union. Putin is not irrational. Already, his Novorossiya project in Ukraine has failed. We should not exaggerate the Russian threat.

At the same time, Putin will take advantage of opportunities, including splits within the alliance or ambiguities about NATO's commitment to defend all members. We must deny him new opportunities, and reduce to zero his doubt about our commitment to defending all NATO allies against military threats. That's why President

Obama made the right decision to dramatically increase the size of the European Reassurance Initiative (ERI) to $3.4 billion. That's why NATO's plan to deploy four battalions on a rotational basis in Poland, Estonia, Latvia, and Lithuania is the right decision to complement a series of decisions taken earlier, including the creation of the Very High Readiness Joint Task Force, to strengthen NATO's deterrent capacity. The United States should participate in one of these deployments and at the same maintain our bilateral military cooperation with all of these countries.

Lift Sanctions (at the Appropriate Time)

The United States and our allies should lift sanctions against Russian companies and individuals immediately after Putin and his surrogates in eastern Ukraine implement the Minsk agreement. Lifting sanctions beforehand would be terribly damaging to American and European credibility. Likewise, a partial lifting of sanctions in return for a partial implementation of Minsk is a dangerous, slippery slope. Sanctions put in place in response to the annexation of Crimea should stay in place until Russia leaves Crimea, however long that may be.

Counter Russian Propaganda

The United States government should not seek to counter Russian propaganda with American propaganda. Instead, the best method for countering disinformation is real reporting from credible journalists in Russia, Ukraine, and other countries in the region. American direct funding of these media outlets would taint them. Instead, our focus should be on providing short-term training opportunities, yearlong fellowships at American and European universities, and internships at Western media organizations. Education and the free-flow of information are our best tools in this long struggle against Russian propaganda.

Work with the Russian Government on Issues of Mutual Interest

Even after Putin decided to portray the United States as an enemy to bolster his domestic support, he continued to engage with President Obama and his administration on a limited set of issues on which our interests overlapped. For instance, during this period of confrontation, our two governments still managed to work together to remove chemical weapons from Syria and to maintain unity in the P5+1 process to achieve an agreement to prevent Iran from obtaining nuclear weapons. When opportunities to cooperate with Russia arise on issues of mutual benefit, we should pursue them, and not link cooperation on these issues to progress on other issues of disagreement.

We should not continue to pursue engagement, however, without results. Putin's military intervention in Syria, for instance, has achieved his goal of shoring up the Assad and his regime, at least in the short-term. The United States has no interest in associating with that objective. If the Obama administration continues to work with Russia on Syria, we must demand more from our Russian counterparts, and push them to pressure Assad to do more, including allowing more humanitarian assistance reach to distressed Syrian communities, and engaging more seriously in a political negotiation process.

Deepen Engagement with Russian Society

Many Russians in the government, business, and society quietly believe that Putin's current course of confrontation with the West does not serve Russia's long-term economic and strategic interests. We should not isolate these people, but instead maintain contact with them. The United States and our European allies should increase efforts to engage directly with the Russian people, including students through exchanges and scholarships, peer-to-peer dialogue with non-government organizations, and allowing Russian companies not tied to the state to continue to work with Western partners. There is no better way to undermine Russian propaganda than a three-week trip to Palo Alto. There is no better way to show that Americans are not obsessed with "destroying Russia" then to send Russian students to spend an academic year in our schools and universities. Likewise, there are no better ambassadors for our country than young Americans studying at Russian universities or interning in Russian companies. The more interaction we can promote between our societies, the better.

Many Russian civil society leaders have been forced to leave Russia. The United States and our allies should increase our efforts to support these people now living in exile, either through scholarships and fellowships to attend universities or work at think tanks, or through direct financial support for their organizations operating from outside Russia.

---

[i] Medvedev's remarks at the NATO summit in Lisbon, at
http://www.nato.int/nato_static/assets/audio/audio_2010_11/20101120_101120f-01.mp3.
[ii] Putin's remarks to the United Russia Congress, November 26, 2011, as cited in Miriam Elder, "Vladimir Putin Rallies Obedient Crowd at Party Congress, The Guardian, November 27, 2011, http://www.theguardian.com/world/2011/nov/27/vladimir-putin-party-congress .
[iii] "Remarks by President Obama to the People of Estonia," Nordea Concert Hall, Tallinn, Estonia, September 3, 2014, https://www.whitehouse.gov/the-press-office/2014/09/03/remarks-president-obama-people-estonia.

Chairman ROYCE. Thank you, Ambassador McFaul.

Now we will go to Ambassador Jack Matlock.

STATEMENT OF THE HONORABLE JACK MATLOCK, FELLOW, RUBENSTEIN FELLOWS ACADEMY, DUKE UNIVERSITY (FORMER AMERICAN AMBASSADOR TO THE U.S.S.R)

Ambassador MATLOCK. Mr. Chairman, members of the committee, thank you for your invitation to join these distinguished scholars.

Chairman ROYCE. Ambassador, I am going to suggest you pull that microphone closer. There you go. Thank you, sir.

Ambassador MATLOCK. All right.

Thank you for your invitation. And I am very pleased to join these distinguished scholars in discussing our relations with Russia. Ambassador McFaul coauthored, among his other works, a fine book which I make a required reading for my students of U.S.-Russian relations. And he, of course, was Ambassador to Russia. And I would have to say that I don't know whether it was an advantage or disadvantage, but he had a larger staff to deal with Russia than I had to deal with the entire Soviet Union. So I don't know whether that was a blessing or a curse, except that I had, I think, the best staff anyone could wish at the time that we were dealing with the Soviet Union. And, of course, Dr. Aron and I go back a long way in many different meetings and so on. So I am very happy to be here along with them.

Some of my perceptions are going to be probably different, because I am deeply concerned with the direction U.S.-Russian relations have taken of late. We can debate—and I will participate in it if we wish—what caused this. I have written extensively on it. And I would simply say that the perception on both sides, in both cases, I think, has distortions. Theirs may be greater or lesser than ours, but there is cause and effect in the interaction that went both ways.

The mutual accusations and public acrimony has at times been reminiscent of that at the height or the depth of the Cold War, but the issues are quite different.

The Cold War was fundamentally about ideology, the attempt of the Communist-ruled Soviet Union to spread its control of other countries by encouraging what Karl Marx had called proletarian revolutions against existing governments. The Soviet leaders called their system socialist, but it actually was state monopoly capitalism that tried to replace market forces with government fiat. It was a catastrophic failure in meeting people's needs, but it managed to build a formidable and, in some respect, unmatched military power.

Today's tensions are not about ideology. Russia is now a capitalist country. Okay, one that has more state control than many others, but basically capitalist. It is not trying to spread communism in the world. Today's tensions, if we really look at them objectively, are more like those that, through incredible misjudgment, brought on World War I—that is, competition for control of territory in and outside Europe.

We know how that ended. Every European country involved suffered more than they could possibly have gained. Competition over territory was bad enough a century ago. Since World War II, however, the danger has risen exponentially if countries with nuclear weapons stumble into military conflict. The number of nuclear weapons that remain in U.S. and Russian arsenals represent a potential existential threat to every nation on Earth, including specifically both Russia and the United States.

So how did we end the Cold War and reduce this threat? One key element was an agreement that President Ronald Reagan and General Secretary Mikhail Gorbachev made in their very first meeting. They agreed on a statement that Reagan had made in two previous speeches: A nuclear war cannot be won and must never be fought. And then they added, since both countries are nuclear powers: That means there can be no war between us.

With that statement agreed, Secretary of State George Shultz was able to argue convincingly that an arms race between us was absurd. We could not fight each other without committing suicide, and what rational leader was going to do that? In just a couple of years, we had abolished a whole class of nuclear weapons and our arsenals and, shortly thereafter, cut strategic nuclear weapons in half.

In concluding the New START agreement, which Ambassador McFaul has reminded us of, the Obama administration made an important contribution to our national security. But, since then, nuclear cooperation with Russia has deteriorated and seems practically nonexistent. It is urgent to restore that cooperation if we are to inhibit further proliferation. We are unlikely to do so if we proceed with plans to increase our military presence in Eastern Europe.

I am aware that one of our presumptive candidates for President has indicated that he might find some form of nuclear proliferation desirable. I believe that is profoundly mistaken, as is the idea that allies should pay us for their protection. I do not believe we should use our fine military as hired gendarmes to police the world, even if those protected were willing to pay the cost.

These comments, however, do reflect one important truth which we need to recognize, and that is that military alliances can create liabilities rather than augmenting power. When our interests are not closely aligned, an American security guarantee can create a moral hazard. What is to keep an ''ally'' from picking a fight unnecessarily and then expecting Uncle Sam to win it for him? Sounds like schoolyard bullying to me.

I have trouble, to take just one example today, to find much concurrence between American security interests and Turkish behavior. Is Turkey really an ally, or is it a problem? I don't want to single them out—I could use other examples.

Yes, when we have made commitments, we must honor them. But we must be more careful and selective about taking on liabilities. And some of our alliances formed under the different conditions of the Cold War should be reviewed. And I think that, increasingly, I believe you will find, if you question them, your constituents, many of them are worried about our over-military-involvement in the world, about attempts to use our fine military, the best in the world, to solve problems that can't be solved by military

18

means and to carry out tasks that are more in the interests of other countries than they are in the United States.

We must set our priorities, and the highest priority should be the protection and security of the United States of America. The only thing that threatens our existence would be another nuclear arms race that gets out of hand.

Let's bear that in mind, because that is something President Ronald Reagan understood. Yes, he was a heavy critic of communism, but his idea was, yes, we have to stop the Soviet Union from expanding its influence; they have a crazy system. If that is what they want, that is their business. And, as a matter of fact, we didn't bring down communism; Gorbachev brought down communism. It was brought down by internal pressures, and it was brought down by internal pressures when we ended the Cold War and ended the external pressures on the Soviet Union. I think there are lessons here that we have sometimes forgotten.

Now, I have views on how we might deal with Russia on current issues such as Ukraine and Syria, democratization, and human rights and will share them if you wish. I believe there are dignified ways we can reduce tensions with Russia on those issues and others.

However, the main thing we should bear in mind, that is, in confronting the greatest dangers to civilized life in this country, such as terrorism—didn't we have a reminder just 2 days ago in this horrible massacre? Now, if there is any issue that the U.S. and Russia have common interest, it is in fighting terrorism. They are more vulnerable than we are. Sometimes we tend to forget that. And I still don't understand why we have not been able to have more effective cooperation.

So I think the main thing we need to bear in mind is that, in confronting these things, whether it be terrorism, failed states, organized crime, environmental degradation, U.S. and Russian basic interests are not in conflict. As we deal with them, as we must, Russia will either be part of the problem or part of the solution. It is obviously in our interest to do what we can to encourage Russia to join us in confronting them. They are unlikely to do so if they regard us as an enemy or a competitor for influence in their neighborhood.

As I said, we can argue about who is more responsible for the situation, but the fact is that, as you well know, politics is driven by perceptions. And their perceptions are that we have been consistently moving against their interests and trying to encircle them and even trying to interfere in their internal politics.

Yes, President Putin has made many mistakes, many that are not in Russia's interests. But Russia's President, Russia's Government is a matter for Russians to decide. Their scandals are a matter for them to deal with. And I think when we presume——

Chairman ROYCE. Thank you, Professor Matlock.

Ambassador MATLOCK [continuing]. To do this ourselves, that is——

Chairman ROYCE. Thanks for——

Ambassador MATLOCK. Above all, I think we need to return to the position Reagan and Gorbachev set out: A nuclear war cannot be won, must never be fought, and that means there can be no war between us. To act on any other principle can create a risk to our Nation and the world of unimaginable gravity.

[The prepared statement of Ambassador Matlock follows:]

Prepared Testimony
By Jack F. Matlock, Jr.
House Foreign Affairs Committee
June 14, 2016

Mr. Chairman and Members of the Foreign Affairs Committee,

Thank you for your invitation to join these distinguished scholars to discuss the important issue of U.S. relations with Russia. Ambassador McFaul co-authored a fine book which is required reading for my students of U.S.-Russian relations at Duke University. He is also, of course, one of my successors as American Ambassador in Moscow and I am envious that he had a much larger staff to deal with Russia than I 'had for the entire Soviet Union. I have long been impressed by Dr. Cohen's research. He and I once were mutually supportive when we were the only Americans participating in a security conference in Moscow in the 1990s. It is an honor to join them in this discussion.

I am deeply concerned with the direction U.S.-Russian relations has taken of late. The mutual accusations and public acrimony has at times been reminiscent of that at the height (or depth!) of the Cold War. Yet the issues are quite different. The Cold War was fundamentally about ideology: the attempt of the Communist-ruled Soviet Union to spread its control of other countries by encouraging what Karl Marx called "proletarian revolutions" against existing governments. The Soviet leaders called their system "socialist," but it was actually state-monopoly capitalism that tried by replace market forces with government fiat. It was a catastrophic failure in meeting people's needs, but managed to build a formidable—and in some respect, unmatched—military power.

Today's tensions are not about ideology. Russia is now a capitalist country and is not trying to spread communism in the world. Today's tensions are more like those that, through incredible misjudgment, brought on World War I. That is, competition for control of territory in and outside Europe. We know how it ended; every European country involved suffered more than they could possibly have gained.

Competition over territory was bad enough a century ago. Since World War II, however, the danger has risen exponentially if countries with nuclear weapons stumble into military conflict. The number of nuclear weapons that remain in U.S. and Russian arsenals represent a potential existential threat to every nation on earth, including specifically both Russia and the United States.

So how did we end the Cold War and reduce this threat? One key element was an agreement that President Ronald Reagan and General Secretary Mikhail Gorbachev made in their very first meeting. They agreed on a statement that Reagan had made in two previous speeches: "A nuclear war cannot be won and must never be fought." And then they added, since both countries were nuclear powers, "That means, there can be no war between us." With that statement agreed, Secretary of State George Shultz was able to argue convincingly that an arms race between us was absurd. We could not fight each other without committing suicide, and what rational leader was going to do that? In just a couple of years we had abolished a whole class of nuclear weapons in our arsenals, and shortly thereafter cut strategic nuclear weapons in half.

In concluding the New Start agreement, the Obama administration made an important contribution to our national security, but since then nuclear cooperation with Russia has deteriorated and seems practically non-existent. It is urgent to restore that cooperation if we are to inhibit further proliferation. We are unlikely to do so if we proceed with plans to increase our military presence in Eastern Europe.

I am aware that one of our presumptive candidates for president has indicated that he might find some form of nuclear proliferation desirable. I believe that is profoundly mistaken, as is the idea that allies should pay us for their protection. I do not believe we should use our fine military as hired gendarmes to police the world, even if those protected were willing to pay the costs. These comments, however, do reflect one important truth, and that is that military alliances can create liabilities rather than augmented power. The larger an alliance becomes, the more varied will be the security ambitions of its members. When our interests are not closely aligned, an American security guarantee can create a moral hazard. What is to keep an "ally" from picking a fight unnecessarily and then expecting the United States to win it for him? To some degree, this may be happening already. To take just one contemporary example, I have trouble finding much concurrence between American security interests and Turkish behavior.

Yes, when we have made commitments, we must honor them. But we must be more careful and selective about taking on liabilities. And some of our alliances, formed under the different conditions of the Cold War, should be reviewed. Perhaps it is time to have a European commander of NATO and a supportive role for the United States.

I have views on how we might deal with Russia on current issues such as Ukraine and Syria, democratization and human rights, and will share them if you wish. I believe there are dignified ways we can reduce tension with Russia on those issues and others. However, the main thing we should bear in mind is that in confronting the greatest dangers to civilized life in this century such as terrorism, failed states, organized crime, and environmental degradation, U.S. and Russian basic interests do not conflict. As we deal them, as we must, Russia will either be part of the problem or part of the solution. It is obviously in our interest to do what we can to encourage Russia to join us in confronting them. They are unlikely to do so if they regard us as an enemy, or a competitor for influence in their neighborhood.

Above all, however, we must return to the position Reagan and Gorbachev set out: "A nuclear war cannot be won and must never be fought, and that means there can be no war between us." To act on any other principle can create a risk to our nation—and the world—of unimaginable gravity.

———————

Chairman ROYCE. Thank you for those points.

We now go to Dr. Aron.

STATEMENT OF LEON ARON, PH.D., RESIDENT SCHOLAR AND DIRECTOR OF RUSSIAN STUDIES, THE AMERICAN ENTERPRISE INSTITUTE

Mr. ARON. Thank you very much, Mr. Chairman.

Mr. Chairman, Ranking Member, members of the committee, I don't have to remind anyone in this room that this is a tough, even rough, patch in the relations between the United States and Russia. There are many reasons for this troubling state of affairs, for which both sides bear responsibility.

But I would like to explore today one of the key elements of the present situation, and that is Vladimir Putin's system of beliefs, his vision of Russia in the world, and his understanding of his role as Russia's leader.

I want to do it because, contrary to a fairly popular view, I don't believe that his foreign policy, in particular his relationship with the United States, are made on an ad hoc basis. I think, instead, it is part of a long-term geopolitical project rooted deeply in his ideology, in his self-imposed personal historic mission, and domestic political imperatives of his regime's survival.

There are few tenets in Vladimir Putin's credo that can be fairly ascertained now after his 16 years in power. Whether he was taking a break as the President or not, he was the effective leader.

One, the end of the Cold War was Russia's equivalent of the 1919 Versailles Treaty for Germany, a source of endless humiliation and misery.

Two, the demise of the Soviet Union, in Putin's words, was "the greatest geopolitical tragedy of the 20th century."

Three, the overarching strategic agenda of a truly patriotic Russian leader, not an idiot or a traitor or both, as Putin almost certainly views Mikhail Gorbachev and Boris Yeltsin, is to recover and repossess for Russia political, economic, and geostrategic assets lost by the Soviet state at its fall. A few years back, I called this the Putin doctrine, and I think he has implemented it successfully and consistently virtually from day one of his Presidency.

In addition to his KGB training, these views are also shaped by Putin's favorite philosopher, Ivan Ilyin, whom the Russian President cites in speeches, assigns as reading to governors, and whose remains he had moved from Switzerland to re-inter on one of the most hollowed Russian grounds, the Donskoy Monastery in Moscow.

Ivan Ilyin believed, in essence, that Russia is never wrong but perennially wronged, primarily by the West; the West's hostility to Russia is eternal and prompted by the West's jealousy of Russia's size, natural riches, and, most of all, its incorruptible saintly soul and God-bestowed mission to be the third Rome, the light among nations; the plots against Russia are relentless, and, while truces are possible and often tactically advantageous to Russia, genuine peace with the West is very unlikely.

In addition to ideology—and Mike McFaul referred to this—Putin's foreign policy is also shaped by a large, I would say, urgent and powerful domestic political imperative. By the time of Putin's third Presidency, the toxic domestic economic climate had begun to reduce Russian economic growth to a crawl, even with the oil prices historically high. Most troubling for the regime, Putin's popularity, which was and continues to be a key to the regime's legitimacy, dropped by almost one-third between 2008 and 2011.

In the words of Putin's personal friend, trusted adviser, and former First Deputy Prime Minister and Minister of Finance, Alexei Kudrin, Russia had hit an institutional wall and needed a different economic model.

Putin chose to ignore this advice and reject it. And, instead of liberalizing institutional reforms, he made likely the most fateful decision of his political career: He began to shift the foundation of his regime's legitimacy from economic progress and steady growth of incomes to what might be called patriotic mobilization. There followed the annexation of Crimea, the hybrid war in Ukraine, and then Russia's involvement in Syria.

Putin appears to have stepped on an authoritarian escalator from which there is no exit except by physical demise or revolution. And the regime he is heading is presenting the West with an unprecedented challenge: A highly personalistic authoritarianism, which is resurgent, activist, inspired by a mission, prone to risky behavior both for ideological reasons and for those of domestic political legitimacy, and armed, by the latest count, with 1,735 strategic nuclear warheads on 521 delivery platforms.

Does that mean that the United States cannot cooperate with Putin's Russia? Of course not, so long as we do not waste time and effort in areas where the gap in ultimate goals between Washington and Moscow is too wide to bridge, such as it is, I think, in Syria.

Yet there is one area where the coincidence of goals is not just possible but vital to the interests of the United States. Today, Russia does indeed find itself under siege—of course, not by the West, despite what the state propaganda machine asserts on national television daily. It is under the siege from what, in Mr. Rohrabacher's subcommittee a few months ago, I described as the Russian jihad.

Russia is indeed under pressure domestically and from the outside. And I will be happy to provide you with the results of my research, but let me just mention that we can and should cooperate with Moscow in Central Asia. Central Asia is more vulnerable to Taliban and ISIS than any other region in the world today. Yes, it is primarily Russia's problem, yet it will be our problem, as well, when an area with a population of 68 million people becomes a terrorist haven and a magnet for would-be world jihadists.

Mr. Chairman, in conclusion, I would like to ask that a recent article of mine in Foreign Policy titled ''Playing Tic-Tac-Toe with Putin'' is entered into the record.

Thank you very much.

[The prepared statement of Mr. Aron follows:]

Statement before the House Committee on Foreign Affairs
On US Policy toward Putin's Russia

Drivers of Putin's Foreign Policy

Leon Aron, Ph.D.

Resident Scholar and Director of Russian Studies

American Enterprise Institute

June 14, 2016

Thank you, Mr. Chairman.

Mr. Chairman, the Ranking Members, Members of the Committee!

It is an honor and a pleasure to be here—especially in the company of colleagues and friends whose expertise and integrity I have greatly admired over many years: Jack Matlock and Mike McFaul.

I don't have to remind anyone in this room that this is a tough, even rough, patch in the relations between the United States and Russia.

There are many reasons for this troubling state of affairs, and both sides bear responsibility. But I would like to attempt to explore one of the key elements of the present situation: Vladimir Putin's credo, his vision of Russia in the world, and his understanding of his role as Russia's leader.

I want to do this because, contrary to a rather popular view, I don't believe that his foreign policy, and in particular the regime's relations with the United States, is made on an ad hoc basis. Instead, it is part of a long-term geopolitical project, rooted in deeply held ideology, a self-imposed personal historic mission, and domestic political imperatives of his regime's survival.

The Russian president is not the easiest man to read. They have taught him well in the KGB Higher School and in the Yuri Andropov Red Banner Institute (formerly the Foreign Intelligence Academy). But after 16 years of policymaking, there are a few tenets in Putin's credo we can be fairly certain about:

- The end of the Cold War was Russia's equivalent of the Versailles Treaty for Germany—a source of endless humiliation and misery.
- The demise of the Soviet Union, in Putin's words, was "the greatest geopolitical tragedy of the 20th century."
- The overarching strategic agenda of any truly patriotic Russian leader (not an idiot or a traitor or both, as Putin almost certainly views Gorbachev and Yeltsin) is to recover and repossess the political, economic, and geostrategic assets lost by the Soviet state at its fall. A few years back, I called this program the Putin Doctrine, which the Russian president proceeded to implement virtually from Day One of his first presidential term in 2000.

But I believe there is another, broader and deeper basis for the policies of the Putin regime—a set of beliefs that binds many, perhaps most, key political actors in Russia today, especially the cohort close to Putin, the so-called *siloviki*: top members of special and secret services, many of them graduates, like Putin, of the Soviet KGB. They believe—and there is plenty of evidence in their articles and interviews[1]— that Russia is "menaced by an external force" with the "greatest threats coming from NATO and the United States.[2] A West at war with Russia is the staple of the Russian state's propaganda, which is why Putin called the Europe-bound Ukraine "NATO's foreign legion."

---

[1] See, for example, an interview by the former FSB director (and currently the head of the Security Council) Nikolai Patrushev in the FSB magazine *Za iprotiv*, December 22, 2015.

[2] See, for example, Andrei Soldatov and Michael Rochlitz, "Siloviki in Russian Politics," unpublished paper.

In addition to the KGB training, these views are also shaped by Putin's s favorite philosopher, Ivan Ilyin, whom the Russian president cites in his speeches and whose remains he had moved from Switzerland and interred on the grounds of one of Russia's most hallowed grounds: the Donskoy Monastery in Moscow. Like Ilyin, Putin believes that *Russia* is never wrong, but is perennially wronged by the West. The West's hostility to Russia is eternal and prompted by the West's jealousy of Russia's size, natural riches, and, most of all, its incorruptible, saintly soul and a God-bestowed mission to be the Third Rome, the light among nations. The plots against Russia are relentless, and while truces are possible (and often tactically advantageous to Russia), genuine peace with the West is very unlikely.

Following his boss's lead, Foreign Minister Sergei Lavrov stated in a recent article that it is "in the genes" of the Russian people" to defeat "attempts of the European West to completely subjugate Russia, and to deny [Russia] its national identity and religious faith."[3] Consistent with the view of the West's perennial plotting against Russia, Lavrov also contended that World War II was caused by the "anti-Russian European elites [who] had sought to push Hitler to attack the Soviet Union."[4] And today, too, Lavrov continued:

> We see how the US and the Western alliance it leads try to preserve their dominance by any means possible. . . . The use all sorts of pressures, including economic sanctions and even direct military intervention. [The US] wages large-scale information wars. It has perfected the technology of the change of regimes by implementing "color revolutions."[5]

In addition to ideology, the foreign policy of the Putin government is shaped in large part by a powerful domestic political imperative. By the time of Putin's third presidential term, the toxic domestic economic climate had reduced Russian economic growth to a crawl, even with oil prices at historical highs. Russian economists inside and outside the government warned that, even if oil prices stayed just as high or even climbed higher, the Russian economy would no longer deliver the 8–10 percent growth in real incomes, as it had between 2000 and 2008, securing Putin's astronomic popularity. Public opinion polls consistently revealed people's perception of the authorities at every level as deeply corrupt, callous, and incompetent. Most troubling for the regime, Putin's popularity, which was and continues to be the foundation of the regime's legitimacy, dropped by almost one-third between 2008 and 2011.[6]

In the words of Putin's personal friend, former Deputy Prime Minister and Minister of Finance Alexei Kudrin, Russia's economy by 2013 had hit an "institutional wall" and needed a different "economic model."

---

[3] Russian Ministry of Foreign Affairs, "Статья Министра иностранных дел России С.В.Лаврова «Историческая перспектива внешней политики России», опубликованная в журнале «Россия в глобальной политике» 3 марта 2016 года," March 3, 2016, http://www.mid.ru/foreign_policy/news/-/asset_publisher/cKNonkJE02Bw/content/id/2124391.

[4] Ibid.

[5] Ibid.

[6] Denis Volkov, "Russian Elite Opinion After Crimea," Carnegie Center, Moscow, March 23, 2016.

Yet if Vladimir Putin has a professional or perhaps even personal nightmare, it is likely Gorbachev's perestroika, that is, an effort at economic liberalization that leads to an uncontrollable political crisis and eventually the collapse of the regime.

Unwilling, therefore, to undertake liberalizing institutional reforms, Putin has made likely the most fateful decision of his political career: He began to shift the foundation of his regime's legitimacy from economic progress and the steady growth of incomes to what might be called patriotic mobilization.

The new policy rested on two propaganda narratives. (1) Russia is rising from its knees and because of that the West, first and foremost the United States, declared war on Moscow in order to preserve its *diktat* in world affairs. (2) Although threatened on all sides by implacable enemies, Russia has nothing to fear so long as Putin is at the helm: Not only will he protect the Motherland, but also he will recover the Soviet Union's status of being feared and therefore respected again! On national television, where an overwhelming majority of Russians get their news, foreign policy has become a mesmerizing kaleidoscope of breathtaking initiatives and brilliant successes.

There followed the annexation of Crimea and the hybrid war in Ukraine and then Russia's involvement in Syria.

Thus far, the regime's patriotic mobilization must be judged a great success. A patriotic fervor at the sight of the Motherland besieged yet somehow also victorious; a Russia that again, as in the Soviet days, is mightily shaping world events along with the United States and acting as a moral and strategic counterweight to America has obscured for millions of Russians the increasingly bleak economic reality and repression at home. As the great Russian poet Mikhail Lermontov put it in the poem *Ismail-Bey*, *"Puskay ya rab, no rab tsarya vsellenoy!"*: "Yes, I am a slave but I am a slave of the master of the Universe!"

Vladimir Putin appears to have stepped on the Stalin-Brezhnev-Hussein-Gaddafi president-for-life escalator from which there is no other exit except by physical demise or a revolution. The regime he is heading is presenting the West with an unprecedented challenge: a highly personalistic authoritarianism, which is resurgent, activist, inspired by a mission, prone to risky behavior both for ideological reasons and those of domestic political legitimacy, and armed, by the latest count, with 1,735 strategic nuclear warheads on 521 delivery platforms.

Does this mean that the United States cannot cooperate with Putin's Russia? Of course it does not—so long as the U.S. does not waste time and effort in areas where the gap in ultimate goals between Washington and Moscow is too wide to be bridged. For instance, in Syria, the West wants peace. Putin needs victory. And the victory will likely look like this: The secular, pro-Western opposition is either decimated or forced to disarm as part of the US-Russian "peace process." The Bashar al-Assad regime is saved. The West is confronted with the repugnant choice between Assad, on the one hand, and a combination of ISIS and the al Qaeda affiliate Jabhat al Nusra on the other. Russia, in the meantime, will have been restored to the Soviet Union's position as an indispensable international player and the key outside actor in the Middle East. This certainly would not serve American interests.

Yet, there is one area where the coincidence in goals is not just possible but vital to the interests of the United States. Today, Russia finds itself under siege. Not by the West, of course, despite what the state propaganda machine asserts on national television daily. It is under siege from what I called the Russian Jihad when testifying a few months ago before Mr. Rohrabacher's subcommittee.

I will be happy to go into more details later in this session. Now, let me mention just a few facts:

- Russia has had more prisoners (9) in Guantanamo than any European nation except for Britain, which also has had 9.[7]
- The first and thus far only Taliban commander ever to be tried in a US federal court was a Russian national. Found guilty, he was sentenced on December 3 of last year to life in prison plus 30 years.[8]
- Russia is surpassed only by Tunisia and Saudi Arabia in the number of its nationals fighting with ISIS (2,400).[9]
- Russian-speaking jihadists, from Russia and the former Soviet Union, make up the second largest group of foreigners fighting with ISIS after Arabic speakers[10] (between 5,000–7,000[11]). Russian language graffiti has been spotted in Darayya, Syria ("We will pray in your palace, Putin!" and "Tatars and Chechens, rise up!"[12]), and there is even an Univermag grocery store in the "Russian" district of ISIS's de facto capital of Raqqa, alongside Russian-language schools and kindergartens.[13]

We can't be of much help to Moscow as it struggles to contain the spread of militant Islamism inside Russia. But we can and should cooperate with Moscow in Central Asia, Russia's soft underbelly, to paraphrase Churchill. Next to Afghanistan, Central Asia is likely more vulnerable to the Taliban and ISIS than any other region of the world. The spread of Islamism in Central Asia would bring the Taliban and

---

[7] "The Guantanamo Docket," *New York Times*, http://projects.nytimes.com/guantanamo/country/russia; and Andrew McGregor, "A Sour Freedom: The Return of Russia's Guantanamo Bay Prisoners," Jamestown Foundation, *North Caucasus Analysis*, vol. 7, no. 22,
http://www.jamestown.org/single/?tx_ttnews%5btt_news%5d=3258&no_cache=1#.Va1ElKRVhHx.
[8] Voice of America, "US Sentences Russian Taliban Fighter to Life in Prison," December 3, 2015,
http://www.voanews.com/content/us-sentences-russian-taliban-fighter-to-life-in-prison/3087254.html.
[9] "Foreign Fighters. An Updated Assessment of the Flow of Foreign Fighters into Syria and Iraq," Soufan Group, December 2015.
[10] Mehdi Jedinia, "IS 'Cyrillic Jihadists' Create Their Own Community in Syria," Voice of America, March 30, 2016.
[11] See, for example, Neil MacFarquhar, "For Russia, Links Between Caucasus and ISIS Provoke Anxiety," *New York Times*, November 20, 2015. An estimate by Alexei Malashenko of the Moscow Carnegie Center is between 2,000 and 7,000. Alexei Malashenko, "Что означают последнии теракты для мусульман России" (What the recent terrorist acts mean for Russian Muslims), Carnegie.ru, November 18, 2015. The Soufan group's estimates of ISIS fighters from Russia (2,400) and the former Soviet Republics (4,700) totals 7,100. "Foreign Fighters. An Updated Assessment of the Flow of Foreign Fighters into Syria and Iraq," Soufan Group, December 2015.
[12] "V Tatarstane natsional-speratisty ob"yavili o podderzhke boevikov-islamistov v Sirii" (In Tatarstan national-separatists announce support of militant Islamists in Syria), *Regnum*, June 13, 2013.
[13] Daniil Turovskiy, "Rossiyane protiv Rossiyan v Sirii: Chto izvestno o vykhodtsakh iz Rossii, voyuyushchikh na Blizhnem Vostoke" (Russians against Russians in Syria: What is known about Russian citizens fighting in the Middle East), Meduza, March 28, 2016; and Mehdi Jedinia, "IS 'Cyrillic Jihadists' Create Their Own Community in Syria," VOA, March 30, 2016.

ISIS virtually to Russia's borders—not to mention the hundreds of thousands of Central Asian refugees fleeing to Russia from the Taliban and ISIS if the Central Asian states begin to fall like dominos.

Yes, it is Russia's problem. But it will be Washington's problem as well if an area with a population of 68 million people becomes another terrorist heaven and a magnet for would-be world jihadists.

Again, I'll be happy to discuss the signs and causes of the Central Asian peril as well as how Russia and the United States can work together there. Let me state only that there is a hopeful track record of US-Russian cooperation in trying to stabilize Afghanistan. That experience may be able to inform a joint effort to defend Central Asia from subversion and ultimately a takeover by militant fundamentalism.

Thank you, Mr. Chairman.

———————

Chairman ROYCE. Without objection. Very good. We will enter that into the record, Dr. Aron.

I was going to ask you about your perceptions on Central Asia and where we could cooperate here. And I think your point about recruitment—there are literally thousands of recruits coming out of Russia into ISIS right now, but, on top of that, there is the wider problem of this radicalization and the pace of it.

It seems to me that there is this room for cooperation, but, at the same time, there are questions about what Putin would seek from us, what could he offer. There is also the question in terms of associating ourselves with Putin's counterterrorism efforts, because I am not sure what form they would take, given the way in which we try to conduct our counterterrorism operations with a great deal of, shall we say, care.

And what is, obviously, most vexing to me is watching Syria. Instead of hitting ISIS, he hit the Free Syrian Army, and instead of hitting the army, he hit the markets. His bombers hit, you know, the hospitals, hit the schools. This aspect of this is what is so troublesome for us in the West because it seems counterproductive in terms of the effort of actually going after Islamist terrorism.

So walk us through how, Dr. Aron, we could engage on that front.

Mr. ARON. Well, on Syria, I mentioned, yes, all those things you mentioned could be summarized under the heading of "Different, Divergent Goals." The goal of Putin in Syria is (A) to save the Assad regime, and we could discuss why he wants it; (B) to present the West with a total repugnant choice between Assad and ISIS; and (C) have Russia as the dominant outside player in the Middle East. Clearly, neither of those is our goal.

In Central Asia, on the other hand, I think the goals do coincide. Let me remind you, Mr. Chairman, last week there was not just a terrorist act, there was street fighting in the city of Aktobe in Kazakhstan between government troops and terrorists. That is 400 kilometers from Russia's borders. You know, that is less than 250 miles.

Churchill was mentioned here, I think by Jack Matlock. Central Asia is the soft underbelly of Russia. This is an enormous area. You know that there are 6 million guest workers, many of them illegal, in Russia coming in and out from Central Asia. Russia is the major recruitment center for ISIS, an estimated 300 to 500 recruiters. Most of Central Asians have been recruited not in Kazakhstan or Tajikistan or Kyrgyzstan, they were recruited on construction sites in Moscow to join ISIS.

There are all kinds of statistics. For example, Russian speakers from Russia and the former Soviet Union, primarily Central Asia, are the second-largest language group in ISIS after Arabic speakers.

We cannot help Putin inside the country, and we could discuss why he has this problem inside the country—radicalization of its own Muslims and the guest workers. But in Central Asia, I believe, Tajikistan, Kyrgyzstan, and, to a certain extent, Uzbekistan and Kazakhstan are very troubled states. If they fall, as I said, the danger to us is that they will become havens for terrorists.

Chairman ROYCE. But let me just add a point, because Mr. Engel and I have traveled in Central Asia, and we have had many meetings and many explanations from local government officials about how Gulf-state money floods into that region and acquires either radio stations, television stations, newspapers; increasingly, how also imams come from another part of the world——

Mr. ARON. Right.

Chairman ROYCE [continuing]. And change the indigenous Muslim faith, or ideology, to a new ideology. As they would say to us, these are not our customs, these are customs that are being imported here, but they are changing our culture.

And it looks like what we see happening across Central Asia is also happening across southern Russia. And that, then, leads to this problem. And I would argue this is going to be the next big problem because of the rate at which this is happening.

The last point I wanted to ask you—I am almost out of time—is just some of the stuff that we hear on RT television or in Russian propaganda—the Zika virus was created by the United States. You know, you have a $450 million budget spreading this kind of nonsense across Latin America, Central Asia, Europe, around the world, here, a lot of disinformation, 24 hours a day.

There has to be a more effective way to move forward to counter this disinformation, get the facts out there, and, item by item, knock this stuff down, you know, knock this narrative down with the truth about what is going on, because, obviously, it is having an impact among the Russian-speaking population in Eastern Europe, certainly, but beyond that now. This is being translated in all these other languages. And it is just a constant, big lie, propaganda effort that has to be countered.

Dr. Aron, any response on that?

Mr. ARON. Well, Mr. Chairman, I have to put on my BBG Governor hat. We have a good relationship with your committee. We are working together to make U.S. international broadcasting more effective.

Let me tell you, though, that my own experience is that, ultimately, the most effective countermeasure to the Russian propaganda is not just the U.S. airwaves but empowering the local Russian-speaking population in former Soviet Union.

Chairman ROYCE. Reporters and stringers?

Mr. ARON. Reporters, stringers——

Chairman ROYCE. Uh-huh.

Mr. ARON [continuing]. Through nongovernment and government grants.

One of the examples that I believe I gave, testifying on the issue of the Russian propaganda in the Senate, was StopFake, which is a very effective site in Kiev run by the students of the department of journalism of the Mohyla Academy.

This is ultimately the only way to counter the Russian propaganda, because it gives the people of those countries—and, of course, this could be spread. Similar efforts are occurring in the Baltics and in Central Asia.

Chairman ROYCE. Thank you, Dr. Aron.

Mr. Eliot Engel of New York.

Mr. ENGEL. Thank you, Mr. Chairman.

Ambassador McFaul, I wanted to discuss with you a little bit about one of the things you mentioned when you said that Ukraine is central to blocking Putin.

I have been really at odds with U.S. policy toward Ukraine. First of all, back in 2008, I think it was a strategic blunder that NATO did not admit Ukraine—and Georgia, by the way—in 2008. I know that the Bush administration said that they pushed to have it done but that the Germans and then, to a lesser degree, the French blocked it. I think that Putin's aggression in both those countries would not have happened if they had been members of NATO. I think our lack of bringing them into NATO makes it virtually impossible for them to come into NATO in the future, and I think that was a time lost.

I think that Ukraine is so important. It is really the center of where we have our disagreements with Russia. If we allow Crimea to just be annexed and do nothing about it, don't even talk about it anymore, if we allow Putin to start this nonsense in—if we allow Putin to continue his nonsense, I should say—in eastern Ukraine—you know, reports indicate that the fighting has stepped up again in Ukraine. And it seems that every time Putin feels pressure in one part of the world he will intensify the military campaign in the Ukrainian east as a valve to release that pressure. And, you know, at the same time, Ukraine is fighting serious corruption problems, and it limits its government's ability to respond to the Russian aggression.

I mean, I just think that we have the most pro-Western government in Ukraine that we could possibly have, and God forbid that government falls. It will be 100 years before we will have anything like that.

And, to me, this really strikes at the core of NATO. If we want NATO to continue to be successful and not just worthless, it seems to me Ukraine is where we make our stand.

I disagree with the administration's lack of providing weapons to the people of Ukraine. I know they feel that Ukraine can never beat Russia, and so, if we provide Ukraine with more weapons, it will just escalate the situation. But I think Putin makes a different calculation. When Russian soldiers start coming home in body bags, I think that his calculation will be different, that he can just make trouble whenever he wants to and there will be no price to pay.

So I want you to expand on Ukraine, because I think that is really where it is all about. And shame on us if we allow that regime in Ukraine to falter.

Ambassador MCFAUL. Thank you for the question.

I agree. I agree with everything you just said. I do believe that the best way to support reform and those that care about democracy and markets in Russia is to have Ukraine succeed. I believe that the best way to deter further aggression from Ukraine is to help Ukraine succeed. It is when the government is collapsing, when democracy is not working, when the economy is not producing that creates the permissive conditions for more mischief.

So I really do think the key moment in all of European security right now is what this government will do over the next 2 to 10 years. This is a long-haul issue. This is not something that is going to be solved in 6 months.

Mr. ENGEL. "This government" meaning which government?

Ambassador MCFAUL. The Ukrainian Government.

Mr. ENGEL. The Ukrainian Government.

Ambassador MCFAUL. Yes.

Now, I would disagree slightly. I think there were people that used to be in the government that were better. You know, Minister Jaresko, for instance, was, I think, a great Finance Minister, the former Minister of the Economy. I hope to see them back again.

But, generally, I think the glass is half-full, not half-empty. They are doing some extraordinary things, especially on the macro-economic front, when facing some real big challenges. And, you know, talking to some very senior folks over at the IMF in the last few days, they are pleased with the progress they have made.

The one issue that they agree, that the Ukrainians agree, and I agree that needs more focus is a fight against corruption and to get the oligarchs out of the political process. That is going to be a long process, and we should be engaged in that process. I think what happens in Ukraine really determines the fate of what Russia will do with respect to that part of the world.

With respect to Europe, with NATO, I would just say two things. One, I disagree—I want to make sure everybody understands I do disagree with Ambassador Matlock right now. Whether it was right to expand NATO or not, we could relitigate that. We were probably on different sides of that debate. But to pull back now, I think, would be a very dangerous thing because it would create a vacuum, it would create uncertainty about our commitment to our NATO allies.

And, to me, the best way to keep the peace—we are all quoting Ronald Reagan. Let me quote one more Ronald Reagan quote. I am also at the Hoover Institution, by the way. "Peace through strength." So Putin needs to have zero doubt in his mind that we are going to have our Article 5 commitments to our allies, including our allies the Baltic states and Poland. And that is why I support making that clear.

By the time when we got to the government, just to be clear about the historical record, the debate about Ukraine joining NATO was over. Whether that was good or bad, again, we can talk about that; it was not on the agenda. So when I see on RT that they are doing this in Crimea to stop NATO expansion, it is nonsense. There was no NATO expansion.

I was in the government for 5 years, and pretty much every meeting with Mr. Putin and Mr. Medvedev and on every phone call but one, the issue of NATO expansion never came up once, because the issue was over. Ukraine was not asking to join NATO. NATO did not want Ukraine to join. After the election in 2010, Mr. Yanukovych even more so did not.

It all is a post facto rationalization for what Putin did in Ukraine that he brings that up. And I think we need to be clear about that historical record.

Mr. ENGEL. Okay. Thank you.

Ambassador MCFAUL. Thank you.

Mr. ENGEL. Thank you.

Chairman ROYCE. Thank you.

We go to Mr. Dana Rohrabacher of California.

Mr. ROHRABACHER. Yes. And thank you very much, Mr. Chairman, for making sure that this was a very balanced hearing today. And I appreciate that, realizing that some of the things that I believe are going on in the policies here don't reflect very many of my fellow members' ideas of what the policies should be. But we are all trying to be honest and trying to make a better world, trying to find a way that we can actually have peace between two of these major countries, the United States and Russia.

And I am proud to have played a role in Ronald Reagan's efforts to defeat communism and end the Cold War and, yes, Ronald Reagan's intent to create a new era of friendship between the United States, the people of the United States, and the people of Russia. And I know that Ambassador Matlock played an important role in this, as well, and I am very happy to see him and hear him with us today.

Let me just note, I have been watching this for a long time, as well, and I am appalled at the depth that we have let our relationship sink to at this point. We are at the lowest point of any time since the ending of the Cold War.

And I do not believe, as some people have indicated already that they believe, that all of this can be related to Putin. The fact is there has been an unrelenting hostility toward Russia from the very days that we were negotiating with them and they were making concessions that led to tearing down the Berlin Wall; that led to the withdrawal of Soviet troops, which were no longer Soviet troops, were Russian troops from Eastern Europe; which led to major arms reduction agreements between our countries; that, even during those times, there was an element that hated Russia. Over and over again, we would hear it. And some of them had very good reasons, because their family were murdered by communists, who happened to be Russians, during the Cold War.

And also we had people who just could not get over the fact that it was not Russia that was the enemy in the Cold War, it wasn't the Russian people, but was, indeed, communism that was the enemy. It was the communism that spurred Russia to build these rockets and missiles that threatened us, to support radical elements around the world, to create revolutions in order to establish atheistic communist dictatorships throughout the world. That was communism. That wasn't the Russian people.

But yet there have been thousands of documents that have just recently been declassified—Mr. Matlock, I want to ask you if you have seen some of these and whether you agree with them—that did say that we actually proposed to the Russians that, if they would withdraw their troops from Eastern Europe, that at that point we would not be expanding NATO, and we gave them the impression they would be integrated into the economies of Western Europe and the world. And, in either case, there was no ability for the Russians to get into Europe. That is not even a question. But, at the same time, we end up expanding NATO.

Was there an understanding, although it wasn't written down, that we would not have an expansion of NATO, so that Russians would withdraw their troops and troops with guns aimed at Russia would not go right up to their border? Was that an understanding at that time, Mr. Matlock?

Ambassador MATLOCK. It was indeed. It was indeed the understanding at that time. Now, this was not a legal commitment.

Mr. ROHRABACHER. Right.

Ambassador MATLOCK. I must say I testified in the Senate against the original NATO expansion because I thought it was not in the U.S. interest, and I thought it was not necessary to begin to divide Europe again. At the end of the Cold War, we had a Europe whole and free, and that was the objection. You don't keep a Europe whole and free by taking what had been a Cold War alliance, which should have been preserved as it was, and using it by moving the things left, and it was quite predictable then that if we did.

So the reason that I had for not expanding NATO was the interest of the United States. However, it is quite true that the Bush administration and our allies, particularly our Germans, made statements during German unification that clearly implied that if the Soviet Union did not use force in Eastern Europe, and allow Germany to allow and stay in NATO, there would be no expansion of NATO jurisdiction.

Mr. ROHRABACHER. And this——

Ambassador MATLOCK. At one point, Secretary Baker said not one inch to the east, and Gorbachev answered that, of course, that would be unacceptable. They were talking about east Germany, but the language is general.

Mr. ROHRABACHER. Mr. Chairman——

Ambassador MATLOCK. That was the understanding. Now, it was not a legal question.

Mr. ROHRABACHER. Let me jump in here for a moment. That was long before there was ever any Mr. Putin, and in fact, this is long before any of these ''hostile acts'' that we are being told about happened. That was an indication of what? That people were still going to be treating Russia as if it was the Soviet Union. And so right from the beginning, we have had this incredible hostility that—and just let me note, we have, for example, buzzing our airplanes right now, buzzing—are being buzzed by Russian airplanes, our ships. The American people see that.

Well, where are our ships? The ship that was being buzzed—I don't remember where I heard this—was in the Baltic Sea and here it was, I don't know how many miles from St. Petersburg, but why are we sending our U.S. military forces that close to Russia? We have nuclear weapons delivery systems that are being aimed at Russia. How else would they think of that except as being a hostile act? And for them to buzz a ship to see what kind of ship it was right off their borders.

By the way, some of these ships that we have sent there are closer to Russia than Catalina Island is to Los Angeles. What if some nuclear weapons delivery system showed up there? What would we think? Would we send an airplane out to buzz it around and see what kind of ship it is?

I think that both sides, both Russia and the United States need to take a deep breath and step back from this whole military operation that are actually making things worse rather than making things better, and we need to find out where our differences are, negotiate them, see where we can work together.

And Mr. Aron, thank you very much for your wonderful testimony today, which is aimed at where we need to work together, or we are all going to suffer because radical Islam is the threat today, not the Soviet Union. And so, I appreciate you focusing on where we could cooperate, which would be better for both of us.

So thank you, Mr. Chairman, and——

Chairman ROYCE. Thank you, Mr. Rohrabacher.

Mr. ROHRABACHER. I will be ready for a second round if we have it.

Chairman ROYCE. Okay. And we are going to go to Mr. Gregory Meeks of New York.

Mr. MEEKS. Thank you, Mr. Chairman.

Let me first say, Ambassador McFaul, you are right, and that I have learned a lot listening to all three of you. As you said in your initial statements, it has been very——

Ambassador MCFAUL. And I will send you my book for free, okay.

Mr. MEEKS. Okay. I will take it. I will read it. I have a long trip. It will be good to read. And let me also say that, for me, you know, I consider myself a multilateralist, and I believe that diplomacy is the best way to try to resolve things. And you know, I have heard the conversations going back and forth about President Reagan and Gorbachev. Well, we can always go back to Kennedy and Khrushchev. Even when we were at the height of this danger of nuclear weapons, the dialogue between them continued. In fact, President Kennedy also went to the Soviet Union then to meet with Khrushchev so that they could have conversations, and there were telephone calls going back and forth in trying to make sure that we didn't have a major catastrophic scenario that could have ruined the world actually.

And so, for me, to cast off and say that we shouldn't talk to one country or another just does not make sense in this day and age. It didn't make sense in the 1960s, and it still doesn't make sense today in 2016. And so we have to figure out, in my estimation, on how do we do talk and work with one another. And when I initially came into Congress, with me, there were two huge countries that are important. Sometimes we get along with them and sometimes we don't, but we have got to figure this out.

Russia is one of them. Turkey is the other. Because when you talk about the global context, you can't act as though they don't exist because they do. And so much so, that I was, at that time, tried to establish and we were moving a long a Russian caucus.

We would talk with the Russians on a regular basis and try to get to know members of their Parliament, because sometimes I think when you have parliamentarian-to-parliamentarian conversation relationships, that helps things, as opposed to breaking things down, and I, for one, think that that is a direction that we still need to move in, and I think it is tremendously important.

And as you said, Ambassador McFaul, in this current administration, there is a lot that we have done together, a lot of things. Some, you know, when you talk about the START Treaty and the interest of WTO, security, U.N. Security Council, dealing with, you know, the sanctions against Iran as far as nuclear weapons are concerned because it is all in our mutual interest, and I agree with you 100 percent in regards to supporting and making sure we are there for our NATO allies and not pulling out.

Now, it seems to me, and I just want to be corrected one way or the other, that when Medvedev was in charge, there was really close dialogue, et cetera. Now, some will tell me that Putin was always in charge, and he was the guy in the background. And so when it ended, and Putin came back in, it seemed to me that there then became some real problems with reference to communication, even with reference to you as Ambassador to Russia, and whether or not the reset agreement, whether or not that was successful or not.

Can you tell me what happened? Why, you know, in that change, especially when Putin was in charge all along, what happened right in that period so that our relationships at least try to work in a common interest on things that are common to both of us, what happened in that time?

Ambassador MCFAUL. So Congressman, thank you for that great question that I can't do justice to in a minute-and-a-half, but I think it is a fundamental question, because if we don't get the answer right, the prescriptions are going to be wrong.

I just want to remind you that we did have this period of cooperation, and your efforts, Congressman, I just want to applaud. I think engagement is always good. Even if you disagree, you want to know why you are disagreeing, and somebody—we were talking earlier about cooperation on counterintelligence with terrorists. We did that, Mr. Chairman. We did that with the Russians. And you remember, you and I spent a really interesting day down at the KGB offices, right, learning in terms of cooperation. We were doing all those things.

Moreover, I just want to read you—you don't have to believe. Let me quote President Medvedev speaking about NATO at the NATO summit in Lisbon. I was there with him. This is what he said on the record, and I will tell you what he said after the record later. He said, ''Incidentally''—this is the President of Russia—''even a declaration approved at the end of our talks states that we seek to develop a strategic partnership. This is not a chance choice of words, but signals that we have succeeded in putting the difficult period in our relations behind us now.''

That is the President of Russia. That is not Barack Obama. That is the President of Russia just a few years ago, so you have to explain what happened after that——

Mr. MEEKS. That is right.

Ambassador MCFAUL [continuing]. To understand the conflict. And in my view, just to re-underscore it, it has to do with Putin coming back. Yes, he was the grand decision maker all the time. We dealt with both the Prime Minister and the President when I was in the government, but at the end of day, he had a much more suspicious view of the United States, and in particular, a suspicious view that we go around the world overthrowing regimes, either covertly or overtly that we don't like.

And by way, there is a lot of data to support his hypothesis about American foreign policy over the last 70 years. And so the President—I was at many of these meetings, and the President would sit with Putin and say, The CIA is not supporting the overthrow of Mubarak. The CIA is not supporting the overthrow of your regime. These Russians, some of them are in the back here actually, they are actually acting on their own. These Ukrainians, they are actually acting on their own. They are not controlled by the United States of America.

Putin didn't want to believe that. Now, whether he knew the truth but didn't want to believe it for political purposes or genuinely didn't believe it—we used to argue about that in the administration, but he decided that he needed us as an enemy, to discredit these people.

And the last thing. We have heard—and you know, there is blame to go around, and I am happy to talk about some of the mistakes that we made if I had more time, because I do think we made a few mistakes in the Obama administration. But I want to radically reject this moral equivalency that somehow we are all to blame here, and you know, that it is blame on America, blame on the United States. I want to know precisely what the Obama administration did to cause this conflict, because I can tell you precisely what Putin did.

If we had the 10 Commandments about how to be a good multilateralist, how to be a good international citizen, at the top three, one of them would be: Thou shall not annex the territory of thy neighbor.

And I am sorry, that is what he did.

Mr. MEEKS. That is right.

Ambassador MCFAUL. We didn't annex any territory. We didn't support any revolution against him, and there has to be a response to that. We just can't sit on our hands and say, Well, you know, let's all try to get along here. No, there has to be a response. Thou does not—especially in Europe, we cannot allow annexation to become policy that does not have a response.

Having said all that, I want to remind you that even during the conflict that we had, we still managed to cooperate with Mr. Putin. I was there with him when we did the chemical weapons deal between the United States and Russia in September 2003. That is smart diplomacy. We managed the P5+1 negotiations on Iran, even during this time, and some of these other issues, including terrorism, if we can cooperate where it is in our national interest, we should, but we have to also respond to these aggressive things when they happen.

Mr. MEEKS. Absolutely.

Chairman ROYCE. We are going to go to Mr. Steve Chabot of Ohio.

Mr. CHABOT. Thank you, Mr. Chairman.

Ambassador MATLOCK. Since I was mentioned, may I make a statement here. I have never used moral equivalency. This is not my——

Ambassador MCFAUL. I did not——

Ambassador MATLOCK. Nor have I ever——

Ambassador MCFAUL. I didn't mention you, Jack.

Ambassador MATLOCK. You did.

Ambassador MCFAUL. I didn't mean to.

Chairman ROYCE. If I could——

Ambassador MCFAUL. I was quoting my own testimony.

Chairman ROYCE. If I could go to Mr. Steve Chabot of Ohio, he has some questions.

Mr. CHABOT. Thanks. I have just have a couple of points first before I ask any question. I think it is pretty clear to me and a number of us that I think this administration's withdrawal from America's traditional leadership role has left a power vacuum around the globe, one that Putin has taken advantage of, as well as other bad actors. ISIS, obviously, comes to mind, China building islands in the South China Sea, and then militarizing them.

But Putin, with invading Crimea, and to a great extent, I think the West lamely protested, but ultimately did little or nothing, I would like to commend my colleague from the Commonwealth of Virginia for his attention on Crimea, for example, and my colleague, the ranking member, obviously has stressed in his remarks of Crimea that we not forget what has happened there, because I think the world has to a great extent.

But you know, after basically invading and then having a bogus referendum and essentially taken over the country, they have continued with aggression in eastern Ukraine, and the Ukraines have fought bravely, but they are just outgunned. Putin has also been expanding Russia's military footprint in places like Armenia, which has welcomed thousands of Russian troops and an infusion of advanced weaponry, and this has resulted in Putin pressuring NATO's southern flank, just as the alliance is trying to reinforce its eastern flank, and having been to Poland and Latvia and Lithuania and Estonia and Hungary and other countries in the region, a lot of these countries are just scared to death with what Putin is up to.

But Putin continues to hone in on Nagorno-Karabakh, an area that we don't talk about that much anymore. We talked about it maybe a couple of decades back, but not much anymore, but it is a region that is vulnerable to conflict, and tensions have flared up and deaths are occurring there. There has been military action there in recent months, and I believe he hopes this arrangement, Nagorno-Karabakh will shore up his international reputation and pull Armenia and Azerbaijan closer to Russia and further away from the West.

Putin's engagement in Syria in the Middle East has only complicated matters there. As the U.S. works to defeat a ruthless terrorist group, ISIS in the region, Putin undermines our efforts, to a great extent, by lending support to the Assad regime, continuing to test the limits of Turkey, supplying weapons systems to Iran, and on and on.

But let me—and I don't have a huge amount of time, obviously, even less. Let me go to the first point that I raised about Crimea.

I think that, you know, the world, unfortunately, to a considerable degree, has accepted this as a fait accompli. You don't hear much in the news about it about—in the press much at all. It is my understanding that the repression there is worsening, that Russia is tightening its grip on Crimea, that they are escalating their campaign against dissents, and Dr. Aron, would you comment on what is happening in Crimea and what the rest of the world ought to be doing about it, including the United States now?

Mr. ARON. Well, thank you very much, and I am sure my colleagues could comment, too. Just the latest number by the refugee agency, Ukrainian refugee agency, but I think they are being quite honest here. About 100,000 refugees left Crimea. Now, this is out of a population of probably half a million. What I find most dangerous——

Mr. CHABOT. That is 20 percent of the population has left their country?

Mr. ARON. Approximately. Approximately. I mean, you know, these numbers, because nobody could get there without being harassed, and many are barred from going there, many international organizations by Russia, it is hard to say, but the numbers are staggering.

What concerns me—and I would like to circle back to my issue of the Russian jihad, is that as far as we could establish, in percentage terms, relative to their population, the greatest ethnic representation in ISIS is Crimean Tatars, at between 300 and 500 people, and there are no more than 120,000 Crimea Tatars. Now, this is greatly exacerbated by the fact that Putin dissolved the self-governing body of the Crimea Tatars in Crimea. He prevented their leaders, including Mosad Jamilif, former Soviet dissident, from coming back to their homeland, returning.

So there is a whole group of exiles now in Ukraine. So this all exacerbates the situation, and it, again, feeds into extremism in the case of Crimean Tatars. Because when I spoke about the danger of the Russian jihad, from the inside, the key danger is that the Islamic militancy that used to be confined largely to North Caucasus is now spreading inside Russia. It is spreading toward Tatarstan. It is spreading toward the fringes. Of course, always the fringes, of about 6 million strong Central Asian Diaspora in Russia.

So Crimea, in addition to being a gross violation of international norms, in addition to being a gross violation of human rights of the Crimean Tatars and others who live in Crimea, it is also a very dangerous situation where it could lead to the rise of Islamic extremism.

Mr. CHABOT. Thank you.

Mr. ROHRABACHER [presiding]. Thank you very much, Dr. Aron, and—thank you, and look who has got the gavel now.

Ms. BASS. Oh, oh, we are all in trouble.

Mr. ROHRABACHER. My goodness, isn't democracy wonderful.

I now recognize Karen Bass. Thank you very much.

Ms. BASS. Why, thank you, Mr. Chair.

One, I just wanted to thank the panelists. I really appreciated all the testimony, and I wanted to agree with my colleague here, Representative Meeks, that I am sure all of us learned a lot from what each of you had to say.

I wanted to ask, Ambassador Matlock, you referred to, in your testimony, that you had some additional views on how we could reduce tension. You also said that—I believe you said that one thing that we shouldn't do is increase our military involvement, or require payments from NATO countries, and then you cautioned on taking on liabilities.

And I was wondering, the ranking member is talking about legislation that would impose additional sanctions, and I wondered about your comments within that context, and if we did impose additional sanctions, would that be an example of the liabilities that you were concerned about?

Ambassador MATLOCK. Yes. Thank you very much for the question. Obviously, in just a few minutes, I cannot go into great detail. Let me first address the issue of Ukraine in Crimea.

I think everything said by the others has been correct, but they have taken a lot of things out of context. And frankly, I do not agree that our new national security is significantly affected by what happens in Ukraine. I think we have to have certain priorities. And second, I am certain there is no way to solve the problem militarily. Let's look at reality. Russia, given its history, given its close association, is not going to allow the Ukrainian situation to be solved militarily, so giving military aid, encouraging a military response simply causes more damage to the area, and it is not going to be solved that way.

The basic thing we have to bear in mind, and this is unfortunate, but it is reality, and that is, you cannot have a united prosperous Ukraine which does not have close relations with Russia. And the second thing is, if you look at the politics and history and the economics, Ukraine is better off without Crimea. Now, I don't like the way Russians took it, and we should not recognize it, as we don't. However, to think that by bringing pressure to bear on them we can make them change their policy simply plays into Putin's hands because it makes it a national issue. So any attempts to use military force or to encourage it will make the situation worse.

Now, that is one thing. Now, on the—this is true of some of these other issues. Obviously, terrorism is a threat to both of us. I think that we need to define our aims as to what the ultimate aim is. Our aim in Syria should not be to remove the leader, whoever he is. Our aim should be to do what we can to keep the country from falling apart to keep ISIS out, to keep the refugees out of Europe.

Now, the Russian opinion has been, you will get more chaos in Syria if you remove the current regime the way we did in Iraq, the way we did in Libya. They have a point. Can't we understand that?

Ms. BASS. Can I ask you, if the ranking——

Ambassador MATLOCK. I think what we need to do is to concentrate on those areas where our interests are and find better ways to do them.

Ms. BASS. Thank you.

Ambassador MATLOCK. As far as Russia's internal government, Russians are going to decide that. And to the degree that we try to interfere, they look at it just as we looked at the Communist Party during the Cold War.

Ms. BASS. Okay.

Ambassador MATLOCK. That is if our democratization efforts are simply in opposition to the current regime. They are going to react to that.

Ms. BASS. Let me ask, Ambassador McFaul, I wanted to one question. And thank you very much, Ambassador Matlock.

What do you see as the future? I mean, do you think that Putin is going to make a switch again? I don't know when his "term" is over, but do you think that he will switch again and become the

Prime Minister and prop up another President? What is your best guess?

Ambassador MCFAUL. So first of all, I just want to be clear about this. To the degree that which we interfere, Putin is going to react. I totally agree with Ambassador Matlock on that. What I disagree is the assumption that somehow we are interfering.

We did not give one penny to the democratic opposition when I was in the U.S. Government, and I just want to make that clear because I think you said ''perceptions.'' Well, perceptions have to be rebutted when they are not true, okay. We are not fomenting revolution in Russia and——

Ambassador MATLOCK. But they had an Assistant Secretary of State speaking on a telephone, cell phone that could be monitored talking about who should be the Prime Minister of Ukraine in a revolutionary situation.

Ambassador MCFAUL. I was speaking on——

Ambassador MATLOCK. Now, what are the Russians going to think about that?

Ambassador MCFAUL. Well, that was a mistake. I agree with you.

Ambassador MATLOCK. Not only was it a mistake, it was——

Ambassador MCFAUL. It was a mistake, but if you want to know the full details, it was the mistake in the——

Ambassador MATLOCK. And you wonder about perceptions.

Ambassador MCFAUL. Well, let me give you the——

Ambassador MATLOCK. If it had happened in——

Ambassador MCFAUL. Doctor——

Ambassador MATLOCK [continuing]. Cuba or Mexico, how would we have reacted?

Ambassador MCFAUL. So let me give you the full context of that conversation if you are interested. The conversation was about how to get a coalition government together with President Yanukovych. We, the United States Government, the Obama administration, were seeking to diffuse tensions on the streets, and we, on February 21, worked hard with our European allies to cut a deal between the opposition and Mr. Yanukovych, President Yanukovych. The Vice President called him about a dozen times to cut a deal between him and the street. We were not trying to overthrow Mr. Yanukovych, and 12 hours later, for some unexpected reason, he showed up in Rostov. To this day, I don't know why he fled. So——

Ms. BASS. My question——

Ambassador MCFAUL [continuing]. You said we need context——

Ms. BASS [continuing]. About Putin——

Ambassador MCFAUL. There is little context.

Ms. BASS. Hello.

Ambassador MCFAUL. But I want to come back to your question, Ma'am.

Ms. BASS. Thank you.

Ambassador MCFAUL. I am a giant optimist about Russia. I want to make that clear. I am a huge optimist about Russia. I can't predict when and where, and the interregnum, I have no prediction about, but I, as a social scientist, I study political and economic change around the world, and Russia is a rich country. Russia has a rising middle class. Most Russians want to be integrated into the world, and yes, Russians should be in charge of their own fate. But Russians, all of them, not just Mr. Putin or that regime, and I just don't think those structural forces of change that Russia is going to somehow be the one country that becomes middle income or high—when they become an even higher income country, and be the one country that will not move in this kind of forces for political and economic modernization.

I just have met too many young people that are just like my students at Stanford that just want a normal life. They want a good job, they want to travel abroad, and they want their government to represent them——

Mr. ROHRABACHER [presiding]. Thank you.

Ambassador MCFAUL. And so in the long run, I am incredibly optimistic about Russia. I just don't know how long the long run is.

Mr. ROHRABACHER. Thank you, Mr. Ambassador.

Mr. ARON. Chairman Rohrabacher——

Mr. ROHRABACHER. The Chair will recognize Mr. Joe Wilson of South Carolina.

Mr. WILSON. Thank you, Acting Chairman Dana Rohrabacher. And it is right on point. I have been optimistic about a U.S./Russian friendship. And I have had a number of visits have been very inspiring to me to promote nuclear cooperation, building friendships with the people of Russia from Moscow to St. Petersburg to Novosibirsk and Siberia. I have been very grateful that my home community of Columbia is the sister city of Shiabinsk. I have had wonderful visits. And every time I go, I have been so impressed by the people of Russia, the culture of Russia.

I have had members of the Duma visit our office. They have been welcomed. But sadly, things have not developed like I anticipated. Additionally, in my home community of South Carolina, the midlands of South Carolina, we welcomed a large number of very prosperous Russian Americans to our community. In fact, the Columbia Civic Ballet could be misidentified as the St. Petersburg Civic Ballet, and we welcome the—again, the extraordinary contributions of Russian Americans to our State.

But sadly, the high hopes that I had of mutual benefit cooperation, as you indicated, with growing middle class travel has really been crushed by the aggression that I have personally seen in our extraordinarily brave ally, the Republic of Georgia, and that hasn't been mentioned. That was 2008. And then, of course, the aggression in Ukraine.

With that, Dr. Aron, in April 2016, Russian fighter jets flew within 30 feet of the USS Donald Cook, then flew a Russian interceptor within 50 feet of American reconnaissance aircraft. Could you explain the rationale between such bizarrely dangerous actions on the part of Russia and what can be done by the United States and our allies to curtail such activity?

Mr. ARON. My goodness, that is quite a question. Before I answer, just a factual correction, if I may. I misspoke. The population of Crimea is 2 million people. So 100,000 refugees constitutes about 5 percent, not 20 percent, an important correction.

I am a big believer, and I know—and I know Jack Matlock may not agree with that, but I think Mike McFaul, and I think similarly about these things. I think most of these acts are done for domestic political purposes. The government of 3 years ago, before Ukraine, before anything else, a top Russian political sociologist, whose name I will not mention, just I don't want to get him in trouble, told me, Leon, you know, why are you talking about foreign policy as something separate from domestic? The only thing going for this regime is its foreign policy. This is where the legitimacy is. Russia rising off its knees again, Russia is where the Soviet Union used to be, and Vladimir Putin secured Russia as a great super power again.

We underestimated the appeal that this caused in the hearts and minds of millions of Russians because we underestimated the hurt that occurred when the Soviet Union collapsed. So these singular facts of bringing it to the brink and bringing it to the point is to show domestically that Putin is not intimidated by the United States, that he is ready to take all the necessary means to defend Russia against the danger that may not exist.

I think Mike McFaul and I agree on this. The point is that he is almost forced to act provocatively because that is where his regime support and legitimacy and popularity is.

Mr. WILSON. And, but again, 30 feet, 50 feet, that is ridiculous. The obvious extraordinary loss of life that could occur is so irresponsible, and not in the interest of the people of Russia, or its foreign policy or its military.

Mr. ARON. Sir, as I said in the concluding remarks to my statement, we are facing an unprecedented danger, a risk-prone, highly personalistic authoritarian regime that acts both out of mission and out of ideology. It is pushed toward these types of acts, and that is what scares me the most.

Mr. WILSON. You mentioned Foreign Affairs magazine, and yesterday, General Philip Breedlove, the former commander of European commander and NATO supreme allied commander, had an article that I am confident you probably already read, that America needs to do more to deter the Russian threat. And so I, again, appreciate all of your service, and I thank you very much for being here today. And I yield back to the——

Mr. ARON. Thank you.

Mr. WILSON [continuing]. Acting chairman, of all people, Dana Rohrabacher.

Mr. ROHRABACHER. Well, thank you. Now, let me get this straight. You have a candidate somewhere saying he wants to make his country great again? And then takes over the reigns of power? That could never happen really in a modern society, could it?

All right. It is supposed to be a joke. That was supposed to be funny. All right. We now have Mr. Boyle.

Mr. BOYLE. Thank you, and thank you to all three of the witnesses. I have several things I want to go over, but first, I can't help the irony that we are having this hearing, and literally, in the last 5 minutes, The Washington Post is reporting that according to security experts, Russian Government hackers have hacked the Democratic National Committee to find oppo research that the DNC has, and that is according to our own security experts. So spare me the moral equivalency language that mistakes have been made on both sides.

Second point I would like to make is I know that there are some who want to conveniently take shots at President Obama and the Obama administration over what happened in Crimea, and that somehow if the U.S. President had been stronger, this would have been prevented. Is it Hungary, 1956, President Eisenhower; 1968, Czechoslovakia would have been Lyndon Johnson; 2008, when George W. Bush was President, the invasion of Georgia. Those were previous Presidents, both Democrats and Republicans, who were unable to prevent a Russian premier, or then chairman of the USSR, from acting.

Now, third, that having been said, I want to associate myself with what Ranking Member Engel said in terms of our response now moving forward to support Ukraine. I believe there is more that we can be and should be doing. Clearly, we are in joint operations now with the three Baltic Republics as well as in Poland. I wish that we were doing more, and I am a cosponsor of legislation to do more in Ukraine, and I was hoping that possibly Mr. McFaul, you could speak to that more specifically what we could be doing now to bolster Ukraine and make sure that those who are Western looking succeed, because I agree, that would be one of the greatest things for American foreign policy.

Ambassador MCFAUL. So thank you for your question, and I agree. I want to associate myself with you in terms of that historical record. I think, in terms of Ukraine, I just want to underscore, again, more context, that I don't see consolidating democracy or strengthening markets in Ukraine as anti-Russian. When I was Ambassador, we had this argument frequently with senior members of the Russian Government, and we—our position, our administration's position, was you should be able to join whatever trade agreement you want, whatever treaty you want, as long as it doesn't infringe on other rights and responsibilities that you have in other organizations that you joined in terms of seeking win-win outcomes.

I think the idea of going back to some 19th century idea of spheres of influence makes no sense in the 21st century. The borders, you know, where I live in the Silicon Valley, the idea that somehow borders and geography are what makes countries rich or not is just, you know, that is a very outdated——

Mr. BOYLE. Very retrograde.

Ambassador MCFAUL. Yeah, I want to just really make that clear that this is not an anti-Russian policy that to support Ukrainian democracy or Ukrainian markets. And in that regard, I think the best investment that you all have supported with your support has been to help develop Ukrainian civil society. I think it has been a fantastic success story, that it cannot be done in other countries for other circumstances. But I think the pressure from society to make the government perform is the best way to try to help reform in Ukraine.

And it is working now. It is difficult, it is hard, it is not easy to correct 30 years of oligarchic corrupt capitalism. I want to underscore that. It is going to be a long process. It is going to take some electoral cycles, in my view, to change that, but I think that is the core. Support society, support independent media, and they will put the pressure on the government.

Mr. BOYLE. Let me—since I have time and now less than, in 50 seconds, let me just shift a bit. You know, there is something kind of self-centered in a sense that we always think when foreign policy actor does X, it is somehow because of something that the U.S. did or did not do. I tend to believe that a lot of Putin's actions in Crimea and eastern Ukraine have less to do with any U.S. policy and more to do with Russian domestic politics, and specifically, his standing, and I was wondering if any of you would like to speak to that. Agree or disagree?

Ambassador MCFAUL. Could I just briefly say——

Ambassador MATLOCK. Now——

Ambassador MCFAUL. Go ahead, Jack. Go ahead. I will go second.

Ambassador MATLOCK. I think one thing we tend to forget is that there is only one country that can solve Ukraine's problems, and that is Ukraine. The basic problem is that Ukraine is a deeply divided society.

When I was Ambassador to the Soviet Union, whenever I went to Ukraine, I always gave my speeches in Ukrainian language. I have been following things that happened in Ukraine since I was a high school student and did reporters on the role during the war. I know this country. And I also know that when they got independence, their borders were, to some degree, artificial. Crimea had only been added by fiat without consulting anybody in the 1950s.

Now—and so Ukraine—I went there to advise a group in the late 1990s on national security from—other former colleagues from our National Security Council, we were telling them how we organize our national security. The Ukrainians came back and said: Look, you are talking about foreign policy. Let me show you what our problem is. And they showed the sides of the last election, very evenly divided almost entirely on the west on one side and on the other side in the east and south.

Now—and this is in every election. Also, they had a constitution, which was not a Federal constitution, it was unitary. A President who won maybe by just 1 percentage of the vote named every governor. And you know where the violence started after the Maidan? It started in the west by them taking over the governorships. The corrupt President that they got rid of would never have been elected if Crimea had not been part of Ukraine.

There are a lot of issues here, a very deep history, and the basic problem is Ukraine. Yes, Russia has intervened, just as we take a very close interest in countries to us but——

Chairman ROYCE [presiding]. Yes, Ambassador, but we have run over the time.

Ambassador MATLOCK [continuing]. The fact is the Ukrainians are going to have to solve it.

Chairman ROYCE. Right.

Ambassador MATLOCK. And our involvement tends to have a negative effect.

Chairman ROYCE. Yes, Ambassador. We are going to need to go to Mr. Ted Poe of Texas. Thank you.

Mr. POE. Thank you, Mr. Chairman. Thank you all for being here. Ambassador Matlock, I appreciate the fact that you are so knowledgeable, and you have looked at the whole issue with Russia as a historical point of view starting with really before World War I. I think we need to understand history, especially the way the Russians understand history so that we can move forward.

I am not going to ask you a question, because if I ask you a question, it is like asking you the time, you will tell me how to make a watch, and so I am just going to make a couple of comments.

I never thought I would see the day that in a committee hearing, we would have two former Ambassadors from the same region of the world mix it up together during the committee hearing. I think that is—it is a good thing. I am not being critical.

Ambassador McFaul. It is democracy, right?

Mr. Poe. It is democracy. I think it is a good thing. Let's talk a little bit about Hitler.

The Russians moved into Georgia in 2008. I am always in the wrong place at the wrong time. I happened to be there a week after they invaded, and I saw the tanks up on the hill, and then in the West, we didn't do anything, and the tanks are still there and they have one-third of Georgia.

Crimea, the Russians took Crimea, their little green men, they moved into eastern Ukraine, chairman and I and some others were there right after the Russians came into eastern Ukraine, and they are still there. I just need a yes or no from the three of you.

Are the Russians going to stay in that one-third portion of Georgia, Crimea, and eastern Ukraine? Are they going to stay there or are they going to go home? Are they going to stay, Mr. Ambassador McFaul? Let's start on—I will start on the far left here. Are they going to stay in those areas?

Ambassador McFaul. My prediction is yes. You said one word.

Mr. Poe. One word. It is either yes or no.

Ambassador McFaul. I am a professor. I don't know how to give one word answers. Yes.

Mr. Poe. Ambassador Matlock, just yes or no.

Ambassador Matlock. I think they are going to stay in those enclaves in Georgia, which the Georgians treat it the way the Serbs were treating Kosovo.

Mr. Poe. All right.

Ambassador Matlock. And the problem has been——

Mr. Poe. Mr. Ambassador, excuse me for interrupting.

Ambassador Matlock. Crimea——

Mr. Poe. Crimea, are they going to stay in Crimea?

Ambassador Matlock. Will they stay? Most likely, unless——

Mr. Poe. Answer the question.

Ambassador Matlock. Unless——

Mr. Poe. Are they going to stay in Crimea?

Ambassador Matlock [continuing]. The majority of the people prefer to be in Ukraine. In that case, Crimea will become a liability, and there will be incentive to join with Ukraine.

Mr. Poe. Eastern Ukraine, are they going to stay in eastern Ukraine?

Ambassador Matlock. They would be required to give Crimea autonomy——

Mr. Poe. Mr. Ambassador, just answer the question.

Ambassador Matlock [continuing]. Which now they haven't been. I think a lot of——

Mr. POE. Mr. Ambassador, to stay in eastern Ukraine? The Russians in eastern Ukraine?

Ambassador MATLOCK. In eastern Ukraine, no. I think there was never an intent——

Mr. POE. Dr. Aron, what is your opinion?

Ambassador MATLOCK [continuing]. To take the Dombok. The Dombok——

Mr. POE. I have moved on to the next witness.

Ambassador MATLOCK. But they——

Mr. POE. I have moved on to the next witness, please, sir. I reclaim my time. My time.

Chairman ROYCE. I think just——

Ambassador MATLOCK. They will make sure that there is not an anti——

Mr. POE. I need some help, Mr. Chairman.

Ambassador MATLOCK. In charge of the Dombok.

Chairman ROYCE. I think my hearing is a little impaired, and I am not the only one with the difficulty sometimes of hearing, and so we will go to Dr. Aron.

Mr. POE. Thank you, sir.

Mr. ARON. Yes, on all three until the regime changes

Mr. POE. All right. The only other question I have time for is what do you think the Russians will do next? Where are they going? I think Putin finds an opportunity, he seizes it, and he moves in. People in Russia are nationalistic. His popularity skyrocketed when he went into Georgia and Ukraine. You know, I think he wants to be the next czar of Russia. I think that is probably what he is after, but where do you think they are going to go—Putin is going to move next?

Ambassador MCFAUL. I don't assume that he has a grand plan to go into this place and that place and the other. I think it is incumbent upon us to reduce the opportunities for him to do those things. I think Novorossiya has been a fantastic failure, for instance. What he tried to do in seizing territory in the eastern Ukraine has been a fantastic failure, and it is, in part, a failure because there was pushback. And that is why, you know, I go back to peace through strength. If we make sure that he has no doubt about our commitments to Estonia, Latvia, and Lithuania, that will keep the peace, and that is what I would want us to focus on as a way not because to confront Russia, but to keep the peace on that very precarious border.

Mr. POE. Dr. Aron, what is your opinion, future movement, if any, by Mr. Putin?

Mr. ARON. The most vulnerable is the Baltics, and of them, the most vulnerable, the Narva area between Russia and Estonia. And I agree with Mike, those are three NATO members now, and presumably, that is a deterrent.

But if the domestic situation requires it, I think Putin may try to expose NATO as a paper tiger, and have a great upsurge in domestic popularity. So that is a huge risk.

Chairman ROYCE. We need to go to Mr. Cicilline of Rhode Island.

Mr. CICILLINE. Thank you, Mr. Chairman. Thank you to our witnesses. I had an opportunity recently to travel with my good friend, Mr. Rohrabacher, to Moscow, and one of the meetings we had was at the Voice of America, Radio Free Europe. What I learned was very disturbing. The Russian Government, under the leadership of President Putin, had shut down all of the radio stations. I think there were 30 or so.

There was one station remaining that had a freestanding license, and then the Russian Government passed a law that required, if I am remembering this correctly, that it have the majority Russian ownership, so that license ultimately was revoked as well.

So Ambassador McFaul, it seems to me that in responding to this very sophisticated and very pervasive state-controlled media and propaganda machine, I think, really extraordinary, I think the best estimates are that they spend more than $450 million a year to broadcast to more than 30 million Russian speakers 24 hours a day, 7 days a week. What, if anything, are we doing, can we do to provide information that counters that narrative when the Voice of America and Radio Free Europe are basically precluded from providing information, or maybe that has changed since my visit?

Ambassador McFAUL. So I want Leon Aron to speak to this because he does serve on the BBG board and he knows these issues a lot better than I do, but I do want to just associate myself with what he said earlier in his testimony.

It is difficult for the United States Government to give money to reporters because that immediately will taint them. I know, you know, all the reporters, almost all the reporters in Russia, and if they were here today, the independent ones, they would say do not do that. We can't—we can't take your money. We need to be independent. What we can do is we can provide them with information, we can have strategic alliances with them to provide that, we can provide internships in our news organizations. We, at Stanford University, for instance, we have a Knight Fellowship program where we will soon have the former editor of Oktyabr as a visiting scholar because she was thrown out of her job.

And so those kinds of things, educational programs, I think, need to get much more attention. Because there are lots of, literally thousands of Russians, trying to figure out a way to contribute to their country that are now living in exile. These are the kind of opportunities that we should expand, but what we can do internally, I will let Leon answer that question, if he wants to.

Mr. ARON. Thanks very much, Mike. Thank you, sir. Just a brief comment. Russia is still not Iran or China. Social media are more or less free, and this is where the effort is going, because the generation we will want to affect is the generation of social media. And you know, as far as I know, BBG and the gruntees, that is the radios, are less of radios. They are more of TVs, they are more of Twitter, they are more of social media platforms, and I think there is hope there.

Mr. CICILLINE. Thank you. The second question I have is, one thing we saw a tremendous evidence of was the deterioration of the Russian economy, serious structural problems, falling oil prices, the Ukraine-related sanctions, and it is pretty clear the Kremlin has worked to preempt potential domestic discontent through this distraction of foreign interventions.

And my question really is, with the conflict in eastern Ukraine settling into a stalemate and the Russian military intervening in

Syria last fall, how long can this kind of opportunistic strategy work? And what should we do to prepare against it? Maybe Ambassador McFaul, I can start with you?

Ambassador MCFAUL. So I agree with your analysis, and public opinion poll data out of Russia, even though it is very difficult to get accurate data, also concurs with that. I would just say historically and comparatively, we are not very good at predicting when declines and economic growth or depression leads to political change, and I would just remind you that I would never try to make a prediction based on that. But is there tension around that? Are people asking why are we in eastern Ukraine when, you know, our economic situation is getting worse? That question is being asked more and more there.

My view is we need to stay the course in terms of what the policy is. I want to lift sanctions on Russian individuals and companies. I want to associate myself with that, if and when they do what they have signed up to do and their proxies have signed up to do in Mensk. It is just that simple. If you do this, then the sanctions will be lifted.

I find it very scary when people say sanctions aren't working, so let's lift them, or an idea that is floating around Europe right now, let's do partial sanctions for partial implementations. I think those are very bad ideas. Thank you.

Chairman ROYCE. We have luncheon with the Dalai Lama, so— and without objection, there are a couple of witness statements that I am going to include for the record.

And now we will go to Mr. Tom Marino of Pennsylvania.

Mr. MARINO. Thank you, Chairman. Excellent hearing. Gentlemen, I would like you to be as precise as possible. We all have something to do after this. I have three questions.

Ambassador MCFAUL. I am not having lunch with the Dalai Lama. I wish I were.

Mr. MARINO. I am a former prosecutor. I don't have time for long winded answers. Let's go to number 1.

Ambassador McFaul, Putin obviously has a very big ego. People say to me he wants to be next General Secretary. I disagree with that. I think Putin wants to be the second Peter the Great, and the plan to make Russia a leading power, if not, the leading power with the world. What say you?

Ambassador MCFAUL. I agree.

Mr. MARINO. Great.

Ambassador MCFAUL. But I want Russia to be great, too. I personally think it would be in our national interest for Russia to be great. I do not believe the strategy he is seeking to achieve that objective is a smart one.

Mr. MARINO. Great. Okay. Dr. Aron, Bush's decision not to intervene in Georgia and Obama's decision not to intervene in Ukraine, I see that as signaling to Putin that the United States does not care to get involved in these foreign affairs, and as that, the U.S. will not challenge Putin, or NATO will not challenge Putin, will this allow him or signal to him that he could continue his expansionism?

Mr. ARON. Putin has not been made to pay for his policies, definitely. The benefits, domestic political benefits, far supersede the price that he had to pay, either economically or militarily. There are ways to change this balance. It would require the things that Mike mentioned about Ukraine. I am also for arming Ukraine with strictly defensive weapons—but you're absolutely right. So long as his benefits, his domestic political benefits, exceed, far exceed the price that he pays politically and economically and militarily for his adventures, he will continue.

Mr. MARINO. Okay. And I am taking a gamble here, Ambassador Matlock. Please be very concise in your answer. Will Putin back off if the United States significantly increases its military strength and go back to the belief of Reagan through peace through strength?

Ambassador MATLOCK. I think he is more likely. I don't know that anybody can say precisely what he will do. He may not know. But the danger is, if we confront what he is doing militarily, which as yet, I think does not affect our national interest with military means, he can push us into another nuclear arms race. I think that is what we have to watch, because that is going to be very hard to deal with.

Mr. MARINO. Okay. Good point, Ambassador Matlock. And then Dr. Aron, would you respond to that as well? Do we need to increase our military strength to keep Putin in check? Ambassador McFaul

Ambassador MCFAUL. Yes.

Ambassador MATLOCK. I think——

Mr. MARINO. Sir, Just a minute. Just a minute. I am asking Ambassador McCaul.

Chairman ROYCE. Ambassador McFaul, you are recognized.

Ambassador MCFAUL. My answer is yes.

Mr. MARINO. Okay.

Ambassador MCFAUL. I support everything we are doing leading up to the Warsaw Summit.

Mr. MARINO. And I am sorry, I referred to you as McCaul.

Ambassador MCFAUL. Because you have a Member McCaul.

Mr. MARINO. I know. Dr. Aron.

Mr. ARON. I believe that Putin needs to see some credible signs of paying more for his policies. Whether—I don't think we need to, you know, boost, you know, tremendously our military forces, but we need to look at specific instances where we can credibly threaten Putin to pay a higher price domestically, politically, for his adventures abroad.

Mr. MARINO. Just a little information. I am vice president of the NATO Parliamentary Assembly. I hear consistently, when I am in NATO meetings around the world, what is the United States going to do to put Putin in his place? I think perhaps he is one of the most dangerous people in the world, and gentlemen, I would love individually to have dinner with each one of you. I could learn so much. Thank you very much. I yield back.

Chairman ROYCE. Thank you, Mr. Marino, and I also want to thank the panel, the witnesses here today. We—and Jerry.

Mr. CONNOLLY. Thank you.

Chairman ROYCE. How are you?

Mr. CONNOLLY. Fine.

53

Chairman ROYCE. I am calling—I am going to recognize you. Go ahead.

Mr. CONNOLLY. Thank you, my friend. Thank you, Mr. Chairman. I want to pick up where my friend Mr. Marino left off. I am the head of the U.S. delegation to the NATO Parliamentary Assembly, and I have to say, I heard a lot of stuff from my friend from California and from Ambassador Matlock that would not, in any way, reflect the reality of our NATO partners across the board, with one or two exceptions. Boy, it would come as news to the Baltic republics that the Russians are peace-loving people who are just buzzing our ships in the Black Sea because we are too close to their littoral, because the Russians are buzzing them, and they are guilty of one thing, sovereign independence. That is what they are guilty of.

They are not doing anything provocative. In fact, the very last thing in the world they want to do is anything provocative. Explain that Russian behavior. The illegal annexation of the sovereign territory of the Ukraine, the Crimea, and now the illegal occupation. I was just in the Ukraine. Fighting goes on as we speak. People are dying because of Russian provocation. Russian subterfuge pretending these are Ukrainian nationalists and patriots who they have no control over.

We have already lost one commercial airliner in that conflict. It was almost certainly downed. It was almost certainly downed at the loss of terrible civilian life over the sovereign territory of the Ukraine because of Russian provocation and Russian provocateurs, not Ukrainians, not Americans hating Russia. Russian behavior.

Putin seems to be engaged in some kind of reestablishment of Russian hegemony in some kind of delusional czarist longing for some glorious past that really never existed, and that is very dangerous. It is also dangerous for Putin to misread U.S. resolve and NATO resolve. I worry about that.

History, in the last 200 years of this republic, is strewn with people who made that miscalculation, pushed us too far.

And Ambassador McFaul, I couldn't agree with you more with what you said earlier. That is Russia's responsibility. Maybe we have miscalculated an occasion. And we certainly shouldn't cloud the fact that there are areas of cooperation we appreciate. You know, we cooperate on the space station. We cooperated on JCPOA to a great contribution to world peace, as far as I am concerned. Although many of my friends on the other side of aisle, in fact, all of them opposed it, but it has been 100 percent complied with, and we are grateful to Russian participation and responsibility for at that.

But Putin seems to be pushing all the wrong—you know, the hot buttons with respect to the NATO alliance and to the United States. And I guess I would ask this, Ambassador McFaul: What is it you think Putin is trying to do? I mean, is it a testing of the system? Is it something more than that?

Ambassador McFAUL. So thank you for your question, and I do agree that we need to stand with our allies. I think the idea of four new battalions in the east is the correct thing. Again, those battalions are not going to invade Russia. Come on, let's be honest about this. Only fools would think about doing that, and we are not foolish, but they are there in a defensive posture.

You know, my own view of why he did what he did is very contingent and circumstantial and emotional. I was still Ambassador, right? He didn't invade Ukraine when I was Ambassador. He invaded the day after I left. I want to point that out for the record. But the buildup was there, and it was in response to the collapse of the government in Kiev, right? It was to exact revenge over his ally falling there. It was not, in my view, some grand design to recreate the Soviet Union, and that, therefore, gives me hope that if we——

Mr. CONNOLLY. But let me interrupt you.

Ambassador MCFAUL. Yeah, please.

Mr. CONNOLLY. Again, I just came back from the Ukraine, but I also was in Kurdistan, I was also in Mongolia. My sense in Central Asia is deep anxiety about Russian intentions. There is a sense among those countries that that is precisely what he is up to, that this was not an isolated example.

Mr. Poe and I, the co-chairs of the Georgia caucus, I assure you the Georgians feel that this is about territorial reengagement and reexpansion after a period of contraction under Yeltsin and that period. And so I think there is real anxiety among lots of former eastern countries too and they are looking to our leadership to try to respond to it.

Mr. Chairman——

Chairman ROYCE. And I think on that point, Mr. Connolly, we really want to thank all the members. I want to thank the witnesses here, too. We had a great exchange of information. We may be following up with each of the witnesses here, and Tom Marino may be following up with you on dinner plans. So again, thank you, and we stand adjourned.

[Whereupon, at 12:10 p.m., the committee was adjourned.]

APPENDIX

MATERIAL SUBMITTED FOR THE RECORD

FULL COMMITTEE HEARING NOTICE
COMMITTEE ON FOREIGN AFFAIRS
U.S. HOUSE OF REPRESENTATIVES
WASHINGTON, DC 20515-6128

Edward R. Royce (R-CA), Chairman

June 14, 2016

TO: MEMBERS OF THE COMMITTEE ON FOREIGN AFFAIRS

You are respectfully requested to attend an OPEN hearing of the Committee on Foreign Affairs, to be held in Room 2172 of the Rayburn House Office Building (and available live on the Committee website at http://www.ForeignAffairs.house.gov):

DATE: Tuesday, June 14, 2016

TIME: 10:00 a.m.

SUBJECT: U.S. Policy Toward Putin's Russia

WITNESSES: The Honorable Michael McFaul
                   Senior Fellow and Director at the Freeman Spogli Institute for
                   International Studies
                   Stanford University
                   (Former American Ambassador to Russia)

                   The Honorable Jack Matlock
                   Fellow
                   Rubenstein Fellows Academy
                   Duke University
                   (Former American Ambassador to the U.S.S.R)

                   Leon Aron, Ph.D.
                   Resident Scholar and Director of Russian Studies
                   The American Enterprise Institute

By Direction of the Chairman

The Committee on Foreign Affairs seeks to make its facilities accessible to persons with disabilities. If you are in need of special accommodations, please call 202/225-5021 at least four business days in advance of the event, whenever practicable. Questions with regard to special accommodations in general (including availability of Committee materials in alternative formats and assistive listening devices) may be directed to the Committee.

COMMITTEE ON FOREIGN AFFAIRS
MINUTES OF FULL COMMITTEE HEARING

Day___*Tuesday*___Date___*6/14/2016*___Room___*2172*___

Starting Time ___*10:08*___ Ending Time ___*12:08*___

Recesses | *0* | (___to___) (___to___) (___to___) (___to___) (___to___) (___to___)

Presiding Member(s)

Chairman Edward R. Royce, Rep. Dana Rohrabacher

Check all of the following that apply:

Open Session ☑   Electronically Recorded (taped) ☑
Executive (closed) Session ☐   Stenographic Record ☑
Televised ☑

TITLE OF HEARING:

U.S. Policy Toward Putin's Russia

COMMITTEE MEMBERS PRESENT:

See attached.

NON-COMMITTEE MEMBERS PRESENT:

none

HEARING WITNESSES: Same as meeting notice attached? Yes ☑ No ☐
(If "no", please list below and include title, agency, department, or organization.)

STATEMENTS FOR THE RECORD: *(List any statements submitted for the record.)*

IFR - Rep. Dana Rohrabacher
SFR - Rep. Chris Smith

TIME SCHEDULED TO RECONVENE
or
TIME ADJOURNED *12:08*

_____
Jean Marter, Director of Committee Operations

HOUSE COMMITTEE ON FOREIGN AFFAIRS

FULL COMMITTEE HEARING

PRESENT	MEMBER
X	Edward R. Royce, CA
	Christopher H. Smith, NJ
	Ileana Ros-Lehtinen, FL
X	Dana Rohrabacher, CA
X	Steve Chabot, OH
X	Joe Wilson, SC
	Michael T. McCaul, TX
	Ted Poe, TX
	Matt Salmon, AZ
	Darrell Issa, CA
X	Tom Marino, PA
	Jeff Duncan, SC
	Mo Brooks, AL
	Paul Cook, CA
	Randy Weber, TX
	Scott Perry, PA
	Ron DeSantis, FL
	Mark Meadows, NC
	Ted Yoho, FL
	Curt Clawson, FL
	Scott DesJarlais, TN
	Reid Ribble, WI
	Dave Trott, MI
X	Lee Zeldin, NY
	Dan Donovan, NY

PRESENT	MEMBER
X	Eliot L. Engel, NY
X	Brad Sherman, CA
X	Gregory W. Meeks, NY
	Albio Sires, NJ
X	Gerald E. Connolly, VA
	Theodore E. Deutch, FL
	Brian Higgins, NY
X	Karen Bass, CA
	William Keating, MA
X	David Cicilline, RI
	Alan Grayson, FL
	Ami Bera, CA
	Alan S. Lowenthal, CA
	Grace Meng, NY
	Lois Frankel, FL
	Tulsi Gabbard, HI
	Joaquin Castro, TX
	Robin Kelly, IL
X	Brendan Boyle, PA

EXTRANEOUS MATERIAL SUBMITTED FOR THE RECORD BY THE HONORABLE DANA ROHRABACHER, A REPRESENTATIVE IN CONGRESS FROM THE STATE OF CALIFORNIA

Statement Into a Record Of June 2015 House Committee On Foreign Affairs Hearing: U.S. POLICY TOWARD PUTIN'S RUSSIA

By ANDREI NEKRASOV, documentary director.

One critical point of disagreement between the Russian Federation and the United States involves Magnitsky Act that was adopted by US Congress in 2012. In my professional capacity as a documentary film maker I made a film examining circumstances of Magnitsky events. To the best of my professional abilities to investigate the documents and to interview the people with direct knowledge of those events I came to conclusion that Mr. Magnitsky was not a whistleblower: there is no evidence of him uncovering any fraud, or accusing the police of committing it (prior to his arrest).

In interviews with me and numerous statements in the media Mr. Magnitsy's boss, Mr. William Browder claimed that on **Oct. 7 2008** Sergei Magnitsky had testified at the Russian Investigation Committee and **accused police officers Karpov and Kuznetsov** of defrauding the Russian treasury of 230 million dollars.

That episode, if it had indeed taken place, would be one of the fundamentals of the narrative presenting Sergei Magnitsky as a hero whistleblower who had uncovered a massive fraud and was jailed and killed by the very police had had accused of it. Mr. Browder claimed that as a result of Magnitky's accusing the officers on Oct. 7, he was, **one month later,** arrested and jailed on the orders of the same very officers.

Having initially based my film on that story, and while working on the scene of Magnitsky accusing the officers, I realised that the episode referred by Browder as testifying and accusing the officers, was in fact a police examination of Magnitsky. The transcript of that examination was presented on Bill Browder's websites as the evidence of Magnitsky's accusations.

The transcript contains no accusations and not even a mention of the officers names.

That discovery led me to investigate other statements by Mr. Browder.

Another essential part of his Magnitsky story is the so-called "theft" of Browder's companies which were used to apply for and to receive the fraudulent tax refund. The companies, Browder told me and the numerous media, had been stolen before the fraud.

Mr Browder also claimed that the "company theft" was the subject of **another** whisleblower testimony by Magnitsky. (There would be thus **two** testimonies, before Magnitsky's arrest; the first (June 5 2008) about the company theft, the second (October 7 2008), discussed above, allegedly about the 230 million treasury fraud).

The "company theft" testimony was in fact also a police examination of Magnitsky as a witness in a criminal investigation. In this one Magnitsky does mention the names of officers Karpov and Kuznetsov. This fact has been used by my opponents and some media (in particular Finantial Times and ABC News) as an evidence of inaccuracies in my film.

The "mentioning" of the names, is being confused, innocently, or on purpose, with accusations of the officers. I insist that Magnitsky **did not accuse** the officers of the 230 million dollar before his arrest, and therefore the motive behind the police seeking to have Magnitsky withdraw his testimony was absent.

The mentioning of the names was a part of Magnitsky recounting the story of a search in his offices. One may derive from that story that, according to Magnitsky, the electronic versions of the articles of association of the companies, removed from the offices by the police, could have been used in the dubious re-registration of the companies. (though Magnitsky does not accuse anyone of the "company theft").

In the Browder's narrative only the paper originals, not printouts of files, are necessary to re-register the companies.

As I discovered, and show in my film, the articles of association, either originals or copies, are not essential in the process of re-registration. Moreover anyone can get a copy (a printout) of company documents from a public registry in Russia (as I tell Browder in the film).

Thus even if one considers Magnitsky's "mentioning of the names" of the officers, during one of the examinations, as something close to an accusation, it is devoid of any revelation or evidence value and thus could have not represented any threat to the police, and a motive for a retaliation.

EXTRANEOUS MATERIAL SUBMITTED FOR THE RECORD BY THE HONORABLE DANA ROHRABACHER, A REPRESENTATIVE IN CONGRESS FROM THE STATE OF CALIFORNIA

My name is William Dunkerley. I am a media business analyst and organization development expert based in New Britain, CT. I have extensive in-country experience in analyzing Russian media organizations from top to bottom and in investigating the credibility demonstrated by American media organizations in covering important issues regarding Russia and its leaders. I have several affiliations that are detailed in an appended bio.

Thank you for the opportunity to introduce evidence on the prospects for redirecting today's vitriolic and contentious US-Russia relationship toward areas of productive cooperation.

For many, such a redirection may seem as attainable as finding the end of a rainbow. Every week a battle rages in the media in which America expresses alarm over Russian international aggression and antidemocratic policies at home. In turn Russia expresses alarm over an overbearing US role in the world that includes threats to Russia's security.

My own research and analysis has shown that both sides are pursuing policies that contain a strong element of misunderstanding. I've found that this misunderstanding is propagated to a great extent by misinformation found in the media of the respective countries.

The award winning Stanford University professor emeritus Martin Hellman wrote: "The more I study Russian-American relations, the more potential I see for a misunderstanding to escalate into a crisis, and the more concerned I become about the world's nuclear complacency. I sometimes feel like a German Jew in the early 1930s who has read *Mein Kampf* and tries in vein to alert his countrymen to the need for taking action before it's too late."

I share Hellman's perception of the dangerous potential of entrenched misunderstanding, and strongly believe it mandatory for the Congress to play a leadership role in diverting us from the current perilous trajectory of our approach to Russia.

I will propose a clear and practical plan for accomplishing that. But first I'd like to expand briefly on the facts about the mutual misunderstanding:

For me the misinformation alarm sounded in early 2000. News stories were proliferating that lamented Vladimir Putin's crackdown on Russia's free press. A February 16, 2000 Reuters report headlined, "Journalists say Russia press freedom at risk."

The flaw in that story is that Putin had inherited no free press on which to crack down. I knew that from personal experience with indigenous media organizations. The press freedom story is a fraud perpetrated by two oligarchs. They were engaged in nefarious activities that were frowned upon by Putin. Seeking an upper hand in the matter they used the trumped-up press freedom allegations to compromise him. They were simply seeking an advantage over Putin to protect their own interests. Few people saw through the ruse.

The truth is that Yeltsin era laws precluded the profitability of media outlets. They never had the financial independence to serve their audiences honestly and freely. Their bankrupt condition led them into subjugation by oligarchs, state and private enterprises, governors, mayors, legislators, and even the Kremlin. They all put money into the loss-making media enterprises in return for the ability to color the news to their own favor. I estimate that at least eighty percent of the media were then under the control of some level of government. Close to zero percent were free to reliably tell their audiences the truth.

As a means for citizens to be informed and exercise vigilance over their government, Russia's media were abject failures. Observers who believed the bogus crack-down story had looked only at surface appearances. They seemed oblivious to the fundamental realities, and therefore came to totally unwarranted conclusions. They misunderstood the actual realities. I give greater detail on this consequential problem in my book *Medvedev's Media Affairs*.

The fraudulent tale about press freedom's doom is actually prologue to many stories that were to afterwards.

In early 2007 the International Federation of Journalists commissioned me to study and report on media coverage of the November 2006 polonium poisoning of Alexander Litvinenko. My report to the organization's World Congress documented that the mainstream story accusing Putin of culpability was another fabrication. It was perpetrated convincingly by political enemies of Putin's. Their admitted ultimate aim was to destabilize Russia, foment a violent revolution, and institute a monarchy. That presumably would put them back in control.

Yet still today, after all the foregoing has been publically revealed, the fabrication is regarded not only as the truth, but as proof positive of Putin's criminal modus operandi. I don't know whether or not Putin was involved in Litvinenko's death. My research neither implicates nor exonerates him. But I have proved that those who concocted and advanced that story were lying. This is a very massive and sophisticated scheme that successfully bamboozled the world. I've written two books to document all the details. They are titled *The Phony Litvinenko Murder*, and *Litvinenko Murder Case Solved*.

The widespread misunderstanding created by these misinformation campaigns has led to a serious and untoward consequence. It is a phenomenon known as "confirmation bias." This is a psychological term for people's tendency to interpret information in ways that are in harmony with their existing beliefs, expectations, or hypotheses. It turns out the persistently phony Russia stories have spawned reactions at that level of unshakable belief.

According to Tufts University research professor Raymond S. Nickerson: "If one were to attempt to identify a single problematic aspect of human reasoning that deserves attention above all others, the 'confirmation bias' would have to be among the candidates for consideration. Many have written about this bias, and it appears to be sufficiently strong and pervasive that one is led to wonder whether the bias, by itself, might account for a significant fraction of the disputes, altercations, and misunderstandings that occur among individuals, groups, and nations." Indeed: disputes among nations.

What this means is when information confirms existing beliefs, it results in assigning credibility to that information, even if there is no apparent substantiation. Things that fly in the face of pre-existing expectations tend to be disbelieved.

This is a problem that must be addressed if any significant progress is to be achieved in promoting positive cooperation between the United States and Russia. I strongly urge that Congress address how to disrupt the dangerous downward spiral that's put a death lock on current relations.

Lamentably the information pool about Russia has become so polluted by maliciously-inspired misinformation that we need to start anew in our understanding the country and its leadership.

To that end I wish to advance the following solution:

Congress needs and deserves information on current events that is devoid of confirmation bias. It's been demonstrated that it cannot get that from the Western media, or from governmental, partisan, or commercial sources that have an axe to grind and benefactors to please. Something new is desperately needed.

I recommend establishing a commission comprised exclusively of citizen members that have the skill and expertise to validate or discredit news reports and to supply Congress with authoritative and confidential disclosures.

The commission would function in the realm of observable facts and realism, and not in the domain of ideology. It would be precluded from offering policy advice, and mandated to deal with just the facts on which members of Congress can base their own informed judgments.

Congress should invite Russia as well to set up a counterpart commission so that Russian leaders can have the benefit of their own reality-based information in a similar way.

I realize that the establishment of such a commission would face some critical obstacles. One for instance involves the need to avoid politicization and loading the commission with ideologues. But I have in mind ways to overcome this and other challenges. I'd be pleased to work with Congressional representatives in structuring the commission appropriately.

The United States and Russia are the two nuclear superpowers that uniquely possess the capability to pose an existential threat to human civilization as we know it. This is far too serious a matter to abandon sensibility to reckless partisan or ideological differences. The proposed commission will serve to weed through deceptive media rhetoric, thus avoiding false points of contention. It is our best bet for disrupting the desperate course of deteriorating relations. I urge prompt action on this important matter before it's too late.

Friday 5 February 2016

Six Reasons You Can't Take the Litvinenko Report Seriously

Inquiry points the finger at Vladimir Putin and the Russian state, but its findings are biased, flawed and inconsistent

William Dunkerley

An inquiry into the assassination of Alexander Litvinenko in the heart of London in 2006 has concluded that he was "probably" murdered on the personal orders of Vladimir Putin. This is a troubling accusation.

The report said that Litvinenko, who died from radioactive poisoning, was killed by two Russian agents, Andrei Lugovoi and Dmitry Kovtun, who were most likely acting on behalf of the Russian FSB secret service.

The head of the inquiry, Sir Robert Owen, also came to the conclusion that there was sufficient evidence heard in open court to build a "strong circumstantial case" against the Russian state.

His conclusions mirror those of the late Russian oligarch Boris Berezovsky, who had been living in London waging a campaign against Putin before his own death in 2013. Litvinenko was his chief bomb thrower.

I've been analysing this case since Litvinenko's death, and I've followed the inquiry closely. I don't know whether or not his murder was ordered by the Russian president or anyone in the Kremlin. What I do know is that Owen's findings are not supported by reliable evidence.

The report relies on hearsay and is marred by inconsistent logic. It offers no factual insights into what really happened to Litvinenko, yet has been taken as gospel truth by governments and pundits across the west.

Here are some of the problems:

1. PR Campaign
The inquiry failed to take into account the massive misinformation campaign initiated by Berezovsky. It was Berezovsky, an arch-enemy of Putin, who put forward the narrative that the Russian president was behind the poisoning of Litvinenko and fed this to a gullible western media, with the help of the PR firm Bell Pottinger.

A typical headline of the day was something like "Ex-KGB Spy Murdered on Orders of Putin". No facts were presented, just unsupported allegations. Berezovsky's well-funded management of the public discourse set the tone for everything that was to come. If this had been a jury trial, the media coverage would have prejudiced the case. In the absence of a jury Berezovsky's targets included the public, journalists, police, and government officials. Yet there was no consideration of the impact of this wide-reaching influence in the report.

2. Inconsistent
The inquiry appears to use different evidentiary standards for different witnesses. On the one hand Owen claims that he considers some of the evidence submitted by the two alleged assassins, Lugovoi and Kovtun, to be deficient. As a result, he says, he won't regard as credible any parts of their accounts. But he applies a different standard to others. For example, a retired physics professor named Norman Dombey testified that a polonium sample contains a characteristic fingerprint that allows it to be traced back to its source. However Owen concludes that this fingerprint theory "is flawed and must be rejected". He does not react to problems with some of Dombey's testimony by dismissing all of it. In fact, he says that he received valuable evidence from Dombey.

3. Unreliable
There is also the question of Litvinenko's dramatic deathbed statement implicating Putin that drew so much international attention. Early media reports suggest the statement was composed by Litvinenko himself and dictated to his associate, Alexander Goldfarb. The inquiry report describes Goldfarb as the co-author of the book Death of a Dissident with Marina Litvinenko. It does not mention that he was a close ally of Berezovsky's.

Later media reports quote Goldfarb as saying that he wrote the statement himself and checked it with Litvinenko. Another account suggests the statement was drafted by the family lawyer, George Menzies, and discussed with the PR firm Bell Pottinger, acting for Berezovsky.

Which is correct? And even more importantly, the statement does not explain how Litvinenko could possibly have known of the Russian president's culpability, nor does it offer evidence to back up the allegation.

4. Bias
The report fails to acknowledge that Goldfarb is not an objective observer in this case. For instance, he was also involved in promoting the anti-Putin protests of the punk rock group Pussy Riot. This is important because it suggests that the accusations against Putin form part of a long-running campaign stretching over his entire tenure in the Kremlin. The report recounts many allegations against him as if they were discrete events rather than seeing them as part of a continuous process. The point here is that the inquiry should have considered Goldfarb's testimony within a context of a systematic anti-Putin agenda.

5. Lacking evidence
The report admits that there are no hard facts to support the claims against Putin, noting that "evidence of Russian state involvement in most of these deaths is circumstantial". But "circumstantial" is used here as a euphemism for "factually unsupported". The report goes on to suggest that the other allegations against Putin over the years, for example that he was implicated in the murder of the journalist Anna Politkovskaya, "establish a pattern of events, which is of

contextual importance to the circumstances of Mr Litvinenko's death". In other words, Owen admits to being influenced by unproven cases in his consideration of culpability in Litvinenko's death.

6. Dubious reasoning

The role of Mario Scaramella, an Italian sometimes described as an academic, presented a dilemma for the inquiry. At first Litvinenko publically accused Scaramella of poisoning him to stop him disclosing information about Russia's culpability in Politkovskaya's death. But the story seems to have changed after Berezovsky visited Litvinenko in hospital, after which his people began saying that Litvinenko had blamed Putin. There is no evidence that Scaramella was responsible, but the inquiry accepted a strange reasoning for Litvinenko implicating him in the first place. Apparently the former spy was embarrassed to admit that he hadn't seen Lugovoi and Kovtun as threats, so initially concocted the allegations against Scaramella to salvage his professional pride.

While this analysis points to serious flaws in the report, it does not present evidence to exonerate Putin. As I said, I don't know whether or not he is to blame. But what happened to the presumption of innocence and the need to build a case before declaring someone guilty? It is clear that those who are behind these claims against the Russian president have an agenda, and are using a wealth of means in their attempts to convince others.

The public inquiry's acceptance of so many of their questionable allegations casts a pall over Owen's efforts and renders his report practically useless.

"U.S. Policy Toward Putin's Russia"
Rep. Chris Smith
June 14, 2016

Thank you, Mr. Chairman, for your leadership and for calling a hearing to examine U.S. policy approaches to Russia and Putinism. I also want to welcome our witnesses, and I look forward to their insights on how the United States can most effectively engage with Russia in a way commensurate with our values, our obligations to our allies, and our national interests.

When it comes to values and national security, one is often forced to strike a compromise when it comes to foreign policy, especially since the only 'universal' value we can all agree on is that the security of our own citizens is paramount. With that understanding, we engage in diplomacy in an effort to find that overlap in common interest that allows us at a minimum to peacefully coexist. This is of course a gross simplification, but I make it to emphasize the challenge we face in Putin's Russia: a country guided by leaders who perhaps have more in common with the mob than their Soviet predecessors, and for whom the priority of their own citizens' security is not necessarily a given. Thus they are as unlikely to respond to either modern levers of national power or the old Cold War playbook. And if the mob paradigm is most accurate, is there a corresponding law enforcement approach we can take, when despite many nations' assertions to the contrary, we are not the world's police officer?

The topic of U.S. policy towards Russia is an enormous one, and therefore a challenge to wrap one's arms around it all at once. I find it easier when I personalize it by focusing on my own experience and issues I hold dear. As the Special Representative for Human Trafficking in the Parliamentary Assembly of
the Organization for Security and Cooperation in Europe, I vividly recall raising the trafficking issue at a gathering of parliamentarians meeting in St. Petersburg, Russia in 1999. Despite initially meeting a wall of skepticism and opposition, we ultimately found common ground with Russia's interests to protect its own women and children from such crimes, and thus the issue was incorporated into the OSCE's St. Petersburg Declaration.

Flash forward 17 years later, all of which have occurred under President Putin, and we face a Russia that has banned adoptions of children, which fails to abide by the Hague Convention on Child Abduction, and which has fallen to the third and lowest tier in the annual State Department's Trafficking in Person's report – after sitting on the Tier 2 Watch List for nine years. Where is the common ground here? How do we engage with a foreign leader who continues to ignore the hundreds of thousands of Russian citizens and immigrants who are trafficked within and across its border and who uses his own country's orphans as political bargaining chips in an effort to shield from justice the worst human rights abusers – in this case those who were involved in the torture and murder of Sergei Magnitsky?

This is only one small part of the U.S. foreign policy challenge that is Russia, but it is one that I think personalizes the enormous gap in common values and interests that divide our two nations, and I believe separates much of the world from Russia.